STUDIES IN MINISTRY

EDITORS: G. W. H. LAMPE AND DAVID M. PATON

THE BAPTISMAL SACRIFICE

The Baptismal Sacrifice

GEORGE EVERY
Society of the Sacred Mission
Kelham

SCM PRESS LTD
56 BLOOMSBURY STREET
LONDON

DISTRIBUTED IN
THE UNITED STATES OF AMERICA
BY
ALLENSON — — NAPERVILLE, ILL.

FIRST PUBLISHED 1959
© SCM PRESS LTD 1959
PRINTED IN GREAT BRITAIN BY
THE CAMELOT PRESS LTD
LONDON AND SOUTHAMPTON

THE BAPTISMAL SACRIFICE

'YOU must beware of those who have weakened and diminished the force of baptism . . . You must understand baptism to mean something by which evermore you die and live: and therefore, whether you use the confessional, or any other means of grace, you must still return to the very power that baptism exercises, and begin again to do what you were baptized for, and what your baptism signified. But baptism never does lose its efficacy—not so long as you refuse to despair of reaching salvation. It is true that you may wander awhile from the sign, but that does not make the sign impotent. Although you only receive the sacrament of baptism once, you are continually baptized anew by faith, always dying and yet ever living. When you were baptized, your whole body was submerged, and then came forth again out of the water. Similarly, the essence of the rite was that grace permeated your whole life, in both body and soul; and that it will bring you forth, at the last day, clothed in the white robe of immortality. It follows that we never lose the sign of baptism nor its force; indeed we are continually being rebaptized, until we attain to the completion of the sign at the last day.'

MARTIN LUTHER, *On the Babylonian Captivity of the Church* (1520), translated by B. L. Woolf in *Reformation Writings of Martin Luther*, Vol. I, 1952, pp. 266-7.

CONTENTS

ABBREVIATIONS

Ap. Trad.	*The Apostolic Tradition of St Hippolytus of Rome, Bishop and Martyr*, ed. Dom Gregory Dix. 1937.
Connolly, *Eg.C.O.*	*The So-called Egyptian Church Order and Derived Documents*, ed. Dom R. Hugh Connolly, Cambridge, 1916.
DACL	*Dictionnaire d'archéologie chretienne et de liturgie*, ed. F. Cabrol and H. Leclerq, Paris, 1907-52.
Dix, *Shape*	*The Shape of the Liturgy*, by Dom Gregory Dix, 1945.
EETS	Early English Text Society.
ERE	*Encyclopaedia of Religion and Ethics*, 1908-26.
HBS	Henry Bradshaw Society.
JTS	*Journal of Theological Studies.*
Jungmann	*The Mass of the Roman rite*, by J. A. Jungmann, S.J., Eng. trans., 2 vols., New York, Boston, etc., 1951-2.
Lacey	*Marriage in Church and State*, by T. A. Lacey, revised by R. C. Mortimer for ed. 1947.
L.E.W.	*Liturgies Eastern and Western*, by F. E. Brightman, Vol. I, Oxford, 1896.
Lib. Sacr.	*Liber Sacramentorum*, ed. D. M. Ferotin, Paris, 1912.
Linton	*Twenty-five Consecration Prayers*, trans. with notes by A. Linton, 1921.
Mops.	Theodore of Mopsuestia, *Homélies Catéchétiques*, ed. R. Tonneau and R. Devréesse, Rome, 1949.
M.P.G., M.P.L.	J. P. Migne, *Patrologia Graeco-Latina, Latina.*
Narsai	*The Liturgical Homilies of Narsai*, trans. with an introduction by Dom R. H. Connolly, and appendices by Edmund Bishop, Cambridge, 1909.
Neale and Forbes	*Gallican Liturgies*, ed. J. M. Neale and G. H. Forbes, Burntisland (Scotland), 1855.
Prolegomena	*Prolegomena to the Study of Greek Religion*, by Jane Harrison, Cambridge, 1903.
Watkins	*History of Penance*, by O. D. Watkins, Vol. I, 1920.

PREFACE

THIS book arises in part out of lectures delivered at Lincoln Theological College in 1955, and published in 1957 by James Clarke & Co. under the title of *Lamb to the Slaughter*. In these I endeavoured to interpret the sacrifice of Christ in terms of earlier sacrifices in other religions. Some of the reviewers, especially the Archbishop of York in *The York Diocesan Quarterly*, the Dean of Liverpool in *The Church of England Newspaper*, and a very appreciative reviewer in *The Church of Ireland Gazette*, expressed a particular interest in the liturgical implications. In this book I have therefore pursued further the problems raised by the discovery that baptism and the eucharist are two parts of one and the same mystery, in the hope also of finding answers to some of the questions raised by former students of Kelham, who for many years have perplexed me with posers on the subject of 'indiscriminate baptism'. On this theme I lack the eloquence of Hooker, who in a powerful peroration defended the claims of infants to baptism in emergencies,[1] but it will be clear that I remain on the whole critical of rigorism. Nevertheless I have sufficient sympathy with the difficulties of Christian ministers, faced with parents whose motives for bringing their children to baptism are at most dubious, to suggest tentatively some practical steps whereby the problem might be eased.

To critics in my own community, to Professor G. W. H. Lampe, and above all to the Reverend Robert Symonds for his stimulating conversation on many occasions on this and related subjects, I would wish to express my gratitude.

Acknowledgements for assistance on various points are also due to the Reverend John Maitland Moir, the Reverend John Vincent, Dr Vincent Turner of the University of Manchester, Mr J. D. Ferguson, and to the librarians of the Wellcome Institute, Durham University, and Durham Cathedral.

In the notes and references, where the place of publication is not shown, this is London.

GEORGE EVERY, S.S.M.

[1] *Ecclesiastical Polity*, Bk. V, c. 61, § 5.

CHAPTER ONE

INITIATION AND SACRIFICE

I. DEATH IN LIFE: CIRCUMCISION

RITES of transition, and therefore of initiation into a new stage of development, have a natural basis in the physical process of growth and change through birth, infancy and childhood, to puberty, youth and maturity. All mammals must be weaned and all suffer new changes as they grow older and prepare to mate. Many birds and animals respond to changes in their condition by forms of display akin to dancing, often performed with a regularity and rhythm analogous to that of religious rituals. No doubt in many cases a like regularity, less easily observed, attends the care of the very young. But while animals and birds perform much in their rituals by instinct, and even when bred in captivity, conform to type to a very great extent, the human child learns to talk and walk by imitation and instruction. Lost in the jungle, he may survive, but he cannot become a normal human being. Kept in solitude, deprived of conversation or even of a due measure of affection, his development is distorted. This is no new discovery of modern psychology, although its truth and importance have been impressed upon us by the larger number of deprived children who under better medical attention survive the physical risks of infancy. Human childhood is unique in the animal world as infancy and puberty are not, because the child needs to be brought up, to be introduced into new stages. The problems of childhood, between the nursery stage and adolescence, are those of learning a moral discipline.

Childhood in the narrower sense of the word is not a good time for elaborate rituals. Breeching and going to school will have some celebration, but neither lend themselves to anything long. Therefore as social life and initiatory rituals develop a more complex and delicate elaboration, more will be made of the rituals of birth in symbolic relation to childhood and youth, and more of the rituals of youth, considered as the end of childhood; for within certain limits, a baby is an amenable ritual object, and youths and maidens can be trusted to co-operate with much enthusiasm in rites that mark their transition to full manhood, and blooming into acceptable brides. Little boys and girls are less co-operative. They always want to hurry away and do something else.

Nevertheless, childhood is the real subject of initiation ceremonies. To accept an infant for rearing is to recognize him or her as a potential child. This is not always a matter of course. In great and sophisticated civilizations, in China, Greece, and the Roman empire, as well as in poverty stricken tribes like Bushmen and Australian aborigines, the deliberate exposure of children to death has been, perhaps still is, a recognized social convention. And where infanticide is a crime, it has often been a common crime, a venial misdemeanour in the eyes of public opinion. Human mother-love is not purely automatic or instinctive, but traditional and moral. And where traditions command the rearing of infants the chances against success through many centuries have been very much more than fifty-fifty. When children were accepted, they might refuse to establish themselves, or they might be refused admission into the family by the ancestors, or by the tutelary powers that protect the tribe. Many primitive people believe that the dead return in children, but do not always want to return. They may look again on a cold and difficult world, cry once or twice, and change their mind. If such souls are to stay they must be persuaded, and above all reconciled with all the powers who care for the group, the ancestors, the hearth, the fire on the hearth, the protecting deity or deities. So far the rites of birth relate simply to the establishment of infants. But often there is another element, looking forward to the separation of boys from girls, to the future provision of mothers and warriors. This will appear again in the ordeals of education.

The practice of circumcision is in this context revealing. Most Moslems, and a large number of African and Australasian peoples who may or may not have derived the custom from Islam, circumcise boys in childhood, somewhere between the ages of two or three and ten. The age at which ancient Egyptians circumcised boys is an obscure point, but on the whole the evidence looks in the same direction. Coptic boys are now circumcised at any age between three and ten, and Moslem Egyptians at seven or eight.[1] The evidence of the Old Testament suggests that the original age of circumcision was in childhood,[2] but that the rite had been transferred to infancy at an early stage in the development of what is distinctive in Hebrew religion. Among African and American peoples the movement has been in the other direction, towards the association of circumcision with other ordeals inflicted on potential fathers and warriors at the age of adolescence. These ordeals are often associated with rites to promote fertility, rites rejected by the Hebrew prophets and by those in Israel who clung to the tradition of the wilderness-wandering. It may be for this reason that initiation into the covenant became an infancy-rite.

The use of flint-knives for the operation, not only in ancient Israel, but in Abyssinia and perhaps in ancient Egypt, certainly suggests that the roots of the custom, so far as the Hamitic and Semitic peoples are concerned, reach back into the Stone age.[3] On the other hand the Australian evidence points with more decision to the relative newness of this particular ordeal in Australia, where circumcision had gradually overlaid, and in most places displaced, such older ordeals as pulling out a front tooth, or hairs from particular places. According to Professor A. P. Elkin:[4]

In the central and western use circumcision is the principal ordeal, whereas in the eastern use tooth-knocking, depilation or cicatrization constitute this physical testing and preparation. This eastern use still prevailed in the south-west of Western Australia at the time of white

---

[1] See L. H. Gray in ERE III, p. 662.
[2] E.g. Gen. 17.25, Exod. 4.25; cf. Gen. 21.4 (P), Lev. 12.3. A friend doing field-work in West Africa writes: 'Circumcision defines the hitherto sexless or sex-confused baby as a . . . male child . . . Ewe has the same word for "male" and for "man".'
[3] L. H. Gray in ERE, III, p. 661; cf. Exod. 4.25, Joshua 5.2 ff., George Foucart on circumcision in Egypt in ERE, III, pp. 671-2.
[4] *The Australian Aborigines*, Sydney, 1954, pp. 169-70.

occupation and was never ousted; the western use has only comparatively recently spread to north-eastern Arnhemland, where it is only gradually being integrated into the local culture.

The diffusion of circumcision in Australia may have some bearing on its origin elsewhere. At least it points to a kinship between this and other ordeals symbolizing death in life. Professor Elkin[1] insists that Australian initiation is

normally fashioned on the pattern of the greatest transition rite of all, namely, death; indeed, it is really a pre-enactment of death and of the rising which it is desired should follow death.

Dr Lewis Spence[2] wrote of circumcision among the American Indians as

a symbolical sacrifice of sexuality and type of the surrender of the desires to the religious sentiments; or as a partial sacrifice, symbolical of the sacrifice of the whole body, to a certain deity, which at the same time bound the individual to his god and to his tribal associates by a blood-bond.

Dr L. H. Gray, summing up the significance of circumcision as a whole,[3] wrote with commendable caution:

It is even possible that, despite the variety of motives to which reference has been made, all kinds of circumcision are ultimately reducible not to two causes (sacrifice or sanctification of the reproductive faculties and initiation), but to one, sacrifice; since initiation, with its accompanying austerities, may conceivably be regarded as itself a sacrifice to the tribal deity to obtain admission to the people whom he protects.

This generalization might be applied to other ordeals of initiation besides circumcision. For instance, among the Bushmen 'A girl is put into a tiny hut, made by her mother, with a very small aperture for a door, which her mother closes upon her.' There she is buried, while the women hold dances in her honour.[4] Burial rites, of one kind or another, are common in initiations all over the world. The procession of the initiates at Eleusis explored an underworld whose labyrinths can still be traced under the

[1] *The Australian Aborigines*, p. 166.
[2] ERE, III, p. 670.   [3] *Ibid.*, p. 666.
[4] W. H. L. Bleek and F. C. Lloyd, *Specimens of Bushman Folklore*, 1911, pp. 76-7, cited in I. Schapera, *The Khoisan Peoples of South Africa*, 1930, p. 118.

temple's site. The long winding passages that lead to the cave paintings of the Pyrenees and the Dordogne were very probably trodden by youths who went underground to perform those secret rites that made them free of the hunt. Before they could slay aright the great beasts whose forms are there depicted, they themselves must have a foretaste of death and the underworld.

If we ask the reason why so many initiates are symbolically dead and buried, several possible explanations may be offered. It might be held that they are killed first to escape death afterwards. This explanation would be in line with much in the psychology of primitive man and indeed of the human species. It might explain the anticipation of adult ordeals in the bodies of infants, who are scarred as today they are vaccinated, in the belief that death will not come so near twice for a long time. Or it might be that as Professor Elkin proposes in his account of the Australians, the ordeals of initiation are a rehearsal for death and resurrection through rebirth. Before young men and women endure the real risks of life, they must be prepared for fatalities that may come at any moment. I do not think that these two explanations need be regarded as contradictory. By dying in sign and sacrament death may be both postponed and prepared. But death is not only rehearsed and acted. In these signs someone or something dies, the old man, the young boy or girl, the child, the infant, the old life. To accept responsibility, even the limited responsibility of youth, to become morally accountable, to wear a boy's clothes or be nurse to the babies, is to abjure the tyrannous freedom, the utter irresponsibility of infancy. The baby whose briefest whimper brought mother or sister immediately must accept deposition and discipline, and must indeed die.

Modern psycho-analysis has in certain respects illuminated the significance of this death by insisting on the sexual bond between mother and child. This has brought confusion as well as illumination, in that the sense of sex has been extended, so far as the infant is concerned, to cover a great deal of undifferentiated feeling that is still on the way from sensation to perception as images gradually form. What is probably more important, because more capable of examination, is the light thrown on maternal affection. It is indeed clear that the possessive mother exists and has existed in every culture, and has been far more common than the weakling who shrinks from hazards outside the home. His survival value is slight, but hers may be great. In primitive human groups the mother's power is formidable, since hearth and home are under her direct control. Her share of the larder is gathered within reach of the cooking-pot on her fire, while the men must range abroad, first hunting, and then herding. It may well be that the rigid rules restraining sexual relationships within the family group were devised in the first place to protect boys from their mothers and sisters, and to save mothers and sisters from too close and possessive an attachment to young boys. This the older men, who ranged at a greater distance, would certainly resent, and on their return punish the boys and women. I see no reason to suppose that objections to inbreeding have anything to do with any rudimentary knowledge of social hygiene, or even with an instinct for the preservation of the species. A great deal in the tables of kindred and affinity observed by such primitive peoples as Australian aborigines could not be, by any stretch of argument, represented as of any use from the biological standpoint. Often for instance marriage between cousins on the father's side is commanded, while cousins on the mother's side are forbidden to marry. Moreover in Australia great strictness in these matters coincides with ignorance or oblivion of the part played by sex in procreation.

The truth is that passion is much more obvious than any relation between paternity and childbirth. The fear of passion, not concern for the race, is the root of taboos on incest that are certainly universal in human societies, and only less certainly, though not improbably, absent from animal groups. Our human, moral concern is to avoid quarrelling by insisting that partners in this powerful and dangerous passion must be taken from outside the group and introduced by someone who from first to last will be responsible for them, whether the husband marries into his wife's hearth, or takes his wife to the hearth of his own group.

This is important for our subject in so far as it points to the specifically human understanding of the change from infancy to youth. The human infant is a passionate person, free and indeed encouraged to be indiscriminate in his affections as between his mother and sisters, but attached in the first place to his mother's breast, where her passion for him is allowed free rein. The boy and girl are detached to a greater and lesser extent from her, and also from one another, with a view to their future engagement outside the family group. The rituals of initiation are directed to the discipline of affection, and to the death of the demanding self who insists on a mother's love and a sister's servile attention.

2. SIN AND SACRIFICE

This demanding self, this all-devouring infant, has what the theologians call original sin. This subsists after initiation. The continued presence of concupiscence, of the desire for everything, of unregenerate wishes after the death of 'the old man', is a problem not peculiar to Christendom, but one that at least has analogies in other religions, in that 'the old man', though formally and ritually expelled in baptism or in some other form of initiation, performed with all the right incantations and with the assistance of divine powers, persists in returning.

In this, which is not the only sense or the whole sense of original sin, sin and the fallen state of man is a problem in every religion. Religion itself may be said to arise from the need of ritual reinforcement for moral impulses in view of the unquestionable fact that morality is not instinctive. If parents and children submitted to no moral discipline in their mutual relations, but left all to their natural feelings, chaos, not free affection, would result. Not many children would be deliberately murdered, but while some might be deserted, many more would be devoured by passions within the family. This is the problem raised for humanity by conscious childhood, by the very persistence of human growth.

Morality may be regarded as a primeval revelation of the necessity of discipline, of the obedience of children to parents, or at least to mothers and uncles, and of all, including the mothers, to another superior authority within and without the community, whereby the authority of particular human beings is supported, restrained, and controlled. On this basis initiations arise to correct what appears to be at fault in our natural impulses, and to make us obedient to God, to the tribe, to traditions, good hunters, good shepherds, good ploughmen, good mothers and nurses. Revelation may be a question-begging term, but at this stage in the argument it is not intended to exclude naturalistic explanations of our moral impulses, only to insist that in the order of history, ritual prescriptions come first. Anything that could be called a rationalist, as distinct from a religious morality, appears at a later stage, when the moral impulses have been canalized through generations of religious practice. Moreover, in a rationalist morality the principle of discipline must still apply. The purpose of education is not, as is sometimes fondly supposed, to give free play to all our impulses, but to kill some and release others. However they are killed, the old man and the infant must die, that the young man and the maid may grow.

This is the fundamental object of all ordeals of initiation, not the removal of some impure stain, but the burial of the dead. If this is true of circumcision and of other forms of symbolic wounding to death or burial, it is also true of Christian baptism. The symbolism of this rite has been obscured by the mere sprinkling of a baby's forehead before he or she is marked with the sign of the cross. In the early Christian Church baptism was indeed a bath, but a bath in running water, a dip in the Jordan, a symbolic escape from drowning in the Red Sea, a burial and resurrection with and in the crucified Christ.

These forms of ritual burial are not only sacrificial, but the prototypes of every type of sacrifice. On this point it is now possible to insist without fear of contradiction, as twenty years ago no one could have done. The art of the ice-age, rediscovered and explored in the deep caverns of the south of France and Spain, points unmistakably to the practice of some fairly elaborate rituals underground, in preparation for the hunt, long before the domestication of animals. It is true that we cannot know what parts in these rituals were played by the boys and the older men.

We cannot be certain whether all the paintings were made by experts and shown to the boys as part of their instruction, or whether some were painted by boys in difficult places, in darkness or semi-darkness, from almost inaccessible positions, as tests of endurance in the hunter's business of moving silently and swiftly over difficult country. It may be that the caves were used for rituals by hunting parties before every hunt, or at the opening of the hunting season, as well as in the initiation of the young. But we can hardly be wrong in supposing that the point of going so far underground is to penetrate into the underworld, the land where the dead are buried, and the root of increase for plants, and that the placing of the paintings is partly due to their use in tests of endurance and knowledge.

Henceforth we can safely claim that the making of animal images is older than the ritual slaughter of animals, and that beasts were in some sense sacrificed, offered in figure before the hunt, even in the hunting age. Such votive offerings persist throughout the centuries. I myself have seen in the monastic church of Hosios Loukas in Stiris, in central Greece not far from Distomon and Delphi, a number of small waxen feet offered in supplication to a saint who has a reputation for chiropody. This seems to me a closer analogy to the cave-paintings than to wax images made by witches or sorcerers to be symbolically slain with pins. The art of sorcery presupposes a belief that the manager of rituals is really in control of the situation and can direct the spirits to do his will. It seems unlikely that such self-confidence was very common in the ice age, when prayer for victory against heavy odds suits the situation better. The original animal sacrifices were probably votive offerings of the images of animals, made at initiations or before hunts, in rites where the huntsman's skill was renewed or deepened by contact with the earth and with the dead. The actual slaughter of a particular specimen, for instance a young bear caught and tamed,[1] with all necessary apologies and incantations,

---

[1] By the Ainu in Japan and the Gilyack tribe in Siberia. See Jane Harrison, *Ancient Art and Ritual*, 1913, pp. 92-8, and J. Maringer and H.-J. Bandi, *Art in the Ice Age*, 1953, p. 90, for traces of an analogous ritual at Montespan in the Haut-Garonne.

is a natural development out of this. Sacrifice as we know it in the ancient world, and among most modern primitives, grows up only after the domestication of animals, for the idea of a gift to the gods depends upon the institution of private property. The original idea is rather that the beasts are God's gifts to us in response to prayer, that we must ask permission to use them by making a picture of one, or later by some dramatic action in which a beast is slain, his entrails examined, and portions assigned to gods and men.

In his excellent study of *Nuer Religion*[1] Mr Evans-Pritchard has emphasized the role of sacrificial animals in the life of a Sudanese tribe. Every youth at his initiation is given a bull calf, his 'ox of perfection'.

He plays with it and fondles it. He composes poems about it and gets a small boy to lead it round the camp in the morning or evening as he leaps behind it chanting poems. He walks among the cattle at night ringing a cattle-bell and singing of his kin, his loves, and his cattle, and he praises this ox above all other oxen.

The youth enters through this ox into a new kind of relationship with God, the guardian spirits of his family and lineage, and the ghosts of his ancestors. . . . The ox a father gives his son at his initiation provides him with a direct means of communication with the spiritual world.[2]

Very similar language was used many years ago by a Roman Catholic missionary, Father A. G. Morice, to describe the relationship between his Red Indian friends in the Yukon and their 'animal guardian spirits'. These were not individual animals, but rather archetypes of a species, seen, and sometimes painted, during ordeals of initiation. 'They are the link which connects man with the spiritual world, and the only means of communicating with the unseen.'[3] Sacrificial animals are not in the first place food for the gods, but 'mysterious beings which are in a sense superior to man and nearer to the divine world'.[4]

---

[1] Oxford, 1956, especially pp. 248-71.   [2] *Ibid.*, pp. 251-2.
[3] Cited by J. G. Frazer in *Totemism and Exogamy*, iii, 1910, p. 441. I owe this reference to Christopher Dawson, *The Age of the Gods*, 1928, pp. 35-6.
[4] Christopher Dawson, *Religion and Culture*, 1949, p. 41.

The strength of the bull, the swiftness of the deer, the flight of the eagle, the cunning of the serpent, are revelations of superhuman, and consequently divine, power and glory.

They are killed not only that flesh may refresh our spirits, but to reveal secrets. Even alive they are omens. The flight of birds is watched for information of sun and rain and storm. Horses and geese know many things that are hidden from us. If so it seems probable enough that fresh knowledge may be found in their flesh, as fresh strength comes to us through participation in their power, not only at the dinner-table, but between the shafts of the ploughshare. So long as the animal remains a satisfactory divine image, no objections are made to the sacrifice of animals.

3. MYSTERIES

The idea of sacrifice has developed in the context of pastoral and agricultural life, but it is older than the ploughed field, older than the herd, and will survive both, for its roots are deep in the huntsman's initiation to death, his blooding. We know less of his sister's initiation, but the small maternal figures found in sites of the Aurignacian age, once in the wall of a cave, and older than any other art, might well be votive offerings to Mother Earth from prospective mothers. If so they represent a goddess and her votaries, as the sacrificial beasts represent man to God, and God to man. We know less of women's mysteries in any age than of men's, for most writers have been masculine, and only a few anthropologists, though these among the very best, have so far been women. But a little information on this subject may go a long way, for women's business, and therefore her ritual, has more stability. Men have been huntsmen, shepherds, ploughmen, soldiers and citizens, while women weeded the garden and nursed the children. Men are initiated into occupations, but women into the mystery of being.

Miss Jane Harrison, in her *Prolegomena to the Study of Greek Religion*,[1] has shown us how agricultural rituals grow out of women's mysteries. The mysteries of Demeter at Eleusis, the cult

[1] Cambridge, 1903, especially Chapter IV, pp. 120-62.

of the Egyptian Isis, the worship of the Great Mother in Asia Minor, are such initiations associated with agriculture, gradually drawing in, not only the peasantry, but citizens and rulers fascinated by mystery, until in their latter days they became means of grace, whereby men rather than women, but not men alone, were initiated into something deeper than gardening, corn-growing or child-bearing, into some renewal of generation that would not decay or decline with the death of nations, but might provide a passport to re-establishment not here in the next generation, but in happier fields in another world.

This vision of regeneration in the mysteries of Eleusis is communicated to us through the distorted lens of a hostile critic, citing a document[1] whose precise date cannot be determined, but must be before the last quarter of the second century A.D.:

Following the Phrygians, the Athenians when initiating into the Eleusinian mysteries also show to those who have been made epopts the mighty and wonderful and most perfect mystery for an epopt there —a green ear of corn reaped in silence.

This no doubt is the first shoot of harvest, but

This ear of corn is also for the Athenians the great and perfect spark of light from the Unportrayable One; just as the hierophant himself, not indeed castrated like Attis, but rendered a eunuch by hemlock, and cut off from all fleshly generation,

—(So men must be at the rites of women)—

celebrating by night at Eleusis the great and ineffable mysteries beside a huge fire, cries aloud and makes proclamation, saying: 'Holy Brimo has brought forth a holy Son, Brimos' . . . for holy, he says, is the generation of that which is spiritual or heavenly or sublime, and strong is that which is generated.

The language here is coloured by Christian Gnosticism, as reported by an orthodox critic, but I see no reason to doubt 'a green ear of corn reaped in silence', or 'Holy Brimo has brought forth a

[1] The Ophite (Gnostic) writer quoted by Hippolytus in his *Philosophoumena* (refutation of all philosophies) ed. and trans. F. Legge, 1921, Vol. I, pp. 138-9.

holy son, Brimos'. Miss Harrison accepted both as part of the same liturgical text.[1] She also believed that the holy things revealed at Eleusis were fruits in a basket, called a lichnon, used as a cradle and winnowing fan.[2] These were shown, not only to girls and women, but to all engaged in the mystery of gardening, and in later years as the rite developed a mystical attraction, to those concerned with their inner meaning. So elsewhere the rites of Dionysus, at first conducted only by women votaries, were transformed into Orphic brotherhoods.[3] Most of the mystery religions that spread like wildfire round the Hellenistic world in the last centuries B.C. and the first A.D., were derived in the first place from such rites, or from the worship of a Mother-goddess by gardeners and farmers in Asia and Egypt, the mysteries of Cybele and Isis, whose origins may have been like those of Eleusis. A few, like Mithraism, were mainly male, but this was an occupational religion, a cult for the soldier in his camp on the frontier. The attraction of the mysteries in general lay in their human character, their power to unite men and women of all occupations and backgrounds in cults that were rooted in the experience of childhood.

Tribal and civil religion is moral to this extent, that it does enforce obligations of fellowship, including all the rites required to keep the ground in cultivation, the stock in good condition, the fire burning, the children fed and asleep at the proper time. The sacred marriage, which became the central rite in so many agricultural religions as men and their cattle engaged in the task of fertilizing mother earth, is a marriage between her and them. But in the mystery religions of the Hellenistic world, which were concerned with spiritual relationships between displaced persons, some of them freed slaves, others still in bonds, some discontented aristocrats with their wives and daughters, generally uprooted from the land, and alienated by exile or revolt from their ancestral and civic religions, the sacred marriage was with the earth, conceived as the underworld of death. This is indeed one element in

[1] *Prolegomena*, p. 550.   [2] *Idem*, pp. 519-35.
[3] *Idem*, pp. 389-401, 455-572.

the older rites intended to promote increase, for death is a source of life. But in the mysteries this element was isolated from the ancestral and tribal setting. What was desired was salvation, the new life, a hope of resurrection in another world.

The Christian Church appeared first as another mystery, attached to small, heretical Jewish synagogues, repudiated by the main body of the Jews. In these Christian synagogues proselytes were admitted by baptism, without circumcision, in an unrepeatable initiation, renewed like other mysteries in sacrificial offerings at sacred meals, but never recharged. Nevertheless the effects were remarkable. Christians did live changed lives. By the evidence of their regeneration they changed the world, and supplanted the other mysteries, but in so doing they copied their methods.

Fifty years ago it was common, almost commonplace, to ascribe the origin of the Christian sacraments to the mystery religions. Now their Jewish antecedents are more often emphasized, not only in Christian circles. Resemblances in the details of ritual between Christian baptism and the Jewish baptism of proselytes are at least sufficient to establish the fact that Christian baptismal rites had reached a certain stage of formal development before the breach between Church and Synagogue grew too deep for any mutual borrowing.[1] The great age of Jewish proselytism certainly precedes the growth of the Christian Church, so that the loan can only be in one direction. The two baptisms are like in form but distinct in meaning. It is in the matter of meaning that the resemblance between Christian initiations and those of the mystery religions is most obvious, but in that very resemblance the essential difference appears.

Both are concerned with burying the old man and the unregenerate dead. The difference lies on the other side of death, in the kind of new life that is sought and found. In most of the mystery religions those who came to be initiated sought union with the Mother of all living, desiring to be reborn in another world beyond the tomb, where they might be always and for

[1] See F. Gavin, *The Jewish Antecedents of the Christian Sacraments*, 1928.

ever her infant children. 'As a kid I have fallen into milk' is[1] a cry of triumph found in one inscription.

But the Christian catechumen was crucified with Christ, buried with him in baptism, and risen from the dead prepared for martyrdom. His communion was in honey and milk, but also in sacrificed Body and Blood. In an important sense the Christian religion is nearer to tribal and civic rites than the mystery religions. The Church could, and in the end did provide rites for many nations, rituals of initiation to unite Christians with Christ and introduce them to their social and civic responsibilities. No doubt there were and are disadvantages in this connection between baptism and registration, confirmation and training for adult life, but the very fact that this identification could happen does tell us something of the reasons why the Christian Church conquered the mystery religions in the end of the pagan world. These religions were private mysteries, divorced from social ethics, incapable of conflict with politics and science. If they changed the self, they changed it back into the free flow of fantasy, bringing release from all sense of responsibility, and escape for the time being into an easier world. But Christians took their converts to the cross, and if they did not always carry it, at least they came back better prepared to bear another's burdens.

[1] Recorded in *Prolegomena*, p. 595, cf. p. 584.

CHAPTER TWO

CHRISTIAN BAPTISM

In contrast with our slender knowledge of initiations in the mystery religions and of Jewish proselyte baptism, we have a surprising amount of information about the early history of Christian baptism, so much so that those who consider the sources of Christian rites of initiation are often driven to reconstruct them from the rites themselves. This, as we shall see, is risky.

Our earliest example of a baptismal office is in the *Apostolic Tradition of Hippolytus*, a Roman work of the first quarter of the third century.[1] Another use, with a different order of ceremonies, is prescribed, with fewer details, in the *Didascalia Apostolorum*, which may be safely taken to represent Syrian and Mesopotamian practice before or soon after the Decian persecution of 251.[2] The use in *Hippolytus* corresponds to another description, this time of African provenance, in Tertullian's treatise *Concerning Baptism*, which cannot have been written after 206.[3] Where the two uses agree the *Didache*, which may be older than any of these,[4] confirms their testimony, and so does the *First Apology* of Justin Martyr, written in the middle of the second century.[5] Syrian uses differ from those attested for Rome and Africa in the place of the bishop's sealing and blessing, and in Syria before, and in Rome and Africa after, the baptism with water. They agree in the provision for exercises of preparation before baptism, and in the close integration of the whole initiation with the eucharist. What are now three sacraments, baptism, confirmation, first communion, were then regarded as one baptism for the remission of sins.

[1] Ed. G. Dix, 1937; also by B. S. Easton, Cambridge, 1934.
[2] Ed. R. H. Connolly, Oxford, 1929.
[3] Ed. J. M. Lupton, Cambridge, 1908, and trans. A. Souter, 1919.
[4] In chapters 8-10. The date of the *Didache* remains a mystery. I do not myself believe that it represents the use of any church.
[5] Edited A. W. F. Blunt, Cambridge, 1911.

I. THE NEW TESTAMENT

In the New Testament, little or nothing is said about preparation for Christian baptism, but something may be implied. Professor Oscar Cullmann contends that the use of the same verb in a number of contexts where the grammatical construction is somewhat forced, points to a term used in a customary question asked before a baptism:

'What doth *hinder* me to be baptized ?' (Acts 8.36).

'Can any man *forbid* water, that these should not be baptized which have received the Holy Ghost as well as we ?' (Acts 10.47).

'John *forbad* him, saying, I have need to be baptized of thee' (Matt. 3.14).

The same verb κωλύειν is used of the little children:

'*Forbid* them not, for of such is the kingdom of God' (Mark 10.14). Other instances are given by Cullmann.[1] If he is right, and the question was raised by the candidate himself, or his sponsor before baptism: 'Is there any reason why I should not be baptized?', this at least points to some scrutiny of qualities except in those instances where the will of the Holy Spirit is immediately manifest. Proselytes to Judaism were examined as to their motives, at least in the period after the fall of Jerusalem in A.D. 70.[2]

S. Matthew,[3] S. Luke,[4] and Josephus[5] agree that John the Baptist demanded evidence of repentance before baptism, and imply that some candidates were rejected. Josephus insists on his view that

baptism would be acceptable to God, if they made use of it, not in order to expiate some sins, but for the purification of the body, provided that the soul was thoroughly purified beforehand by righteousness.

This implies a contrast, not with the baptism of proselytes, but with the many ritual washings of Pharisees and Essenes.[6] Moreover, many passages in the New Testament point to some formal

---

[1] In *Baptism in the New Testament*, Eng. trans., 1950, pp. 71-80.
[2] *Babylonian Talmud, Yebamoth*, 47ab.
[3] 3.7-9.   [4] 3.7-14.   [5] *Antiquities*, xviii, c. 5, § 2.
[6] See Josephus, *Jewish War*, ii, c. 8, §§ 7-10. It does not seem to me certain that all proselytes underwent baptism at this time. See a discussion in the *Babylonian Talmud, Yebamoth*, 46ab.

pattern of Christian instruction, a kind of catechism which might be given before or after baptism.[1] In others the word may, sometimes must apply to the whole ordeal of transition, including this and more than this.

Our Lord himself said, according to S. Luke,[2] 'I have a baptism to be baptized with, and how am I straitened until it be accomplished', and in another place in S. Mark's Gospel,[3] 'Are you able to drink the cup that I drink? or to be baptized with the baptism that I am baptized with?' S. Matthew[4] keeps the cup, but not the baptism. By his time of writing the word had acquired a more exact, and a more limited meaning. I believe that the sayings in S. Mark and S. Luke are our Lord's own, and throw light on the nature of John's baptism, that it was more than a washing, more than a ford through Jordan, a time of testing, a temptation in the wilderness. Our Lord's own temptations had this context, and S. Mark's reference to his being with the wild beasts[5] points to an experience common to many of John's disciples. They also had suffered temptations, and eaten locusts, with or without wild honey.[6]

In this sense of the word our Lord's baptism is his whole ordeal, from the Jordan, through the temptations, to Jerusalem, death, and resurrection. To 'be baptized with the baptism that I am baptized with' is to die and rise again with him. 'As many as were baptized into Christ did put on Christ'.[7] This is in what is now considered the first or third epistle of S. Paul. The theme continues in the Epistle to the Romans:[8] 'We who were baptized into Christ were baptized into his death. We were buried therefore with him through baptism into death: that like as Christ was raised from the dead through the glory of the Father, so we also might walk in newness of life. For if we have become united with him by the likeness of his death, we shall be also by the likeness of his resurrection; knowing this, that our old man was crucified with him, that

---

[1] See, e.g., P. Carrington, *The Primitive Christian Catechism*, Cambridge, 1940, *passim*, and J. N. D. Kelly, *Early Christian Creeds*, 1950, pp. 13-23.

[2] 12.50.   [3] 10.38.   [4] 20.23.   [5] 1.13.
[6] *Ibid.*, v. 6.   [7] Gal. 3.27.   [8] 6.3-7, 11.

the body of sin might be done away, that so we should no longer be in bondage to sin; for he that has died is justified from sin. . . . So reckon yourselves to be dead unto sin, but alive unto God in Christ Jesus.'

In the Epistle to the Colossians[1] this is related to circumcision as well as to baptism, taking up a theme that, as we shall see, had been developed in Galatians: 'Ye were also circumcised with a circumcision not made with hands, in the putting off of the body of the flesh, in the circumcision of Christ; having been buried with him in baptism, wherein ye were also raised with him through faith in the working of God, who raised him from the dead.' A fuller exposition of another aspect of the matter is in an earlier letter, in I Corinthians:

Our fathers were all under the cloud, and all passed through the sea; and were all baptized into Moses in the cloud and in the sea; and did all eat the same spiritual meat; and did all drink the same spiritual drink: for they drank of a spiritual rock that followed them: and the rock was Christ.

After a digression by way of warning, S. Paul continues his main theme:

I speak unto wise men; judge ye what I say. The cup of blessing which we bless, is it not a communion of the blood of Christ? The bread which we break, is it not a communion of the body of Christ? seeing that we, who are many, are one body: for we all partake of the one bread.[2]

Here, I think, the close connection between baptism and the eucharist is already apparent. S. Paul is explicit about the analogy between Christian and pagan mysteries. As 'in one Spirit were we all baptized into one body, whether Jews or Greeks, whether bond or free; and were all made to drink of one Spirit';[3] so therefore 'Ye cannot drink of the cup of the Lord and the cup of devils: ye cannot partake of the table of the Lord, and of the table of devils.'[4] 'For as often as ye eat this bread, and drink this cup, ye proclaim the Lord's death till he come. Wherefore whoever shall eat the bread or drink the cup of the Lord unworthily, shall be guilty of the body and blood of the Lord. . . . For this

[1] 2.11-12.   [2] 10.1-4, 15-17.   [3] 12.13.   [4] 10.21.

cause many among you are weak and sickly, and not a few sleep.'[1] According to these chapters, we are partakers of Christ in baptism and the eucharist, as others think that they partake of tutelary spirits. The physical effects should be more startling, for here is the Lord God, the creator of the world, who has now entered with holy fire into human flesh.

Is this teaching S. Paul's own, and peculiar to him? The charge was made against him, and he had to fight back in the first (or third) epistle of the New Testament. The battle against circumcision, and for justification by faith, is a battle about this.

They desire to have you circumcised, that they may glory in your flesh. But far be it from me to glory, save in the cross of our Lord Jesus Christ, through whom the world hath been crucified unto me and I unto the world.[2]

S. Paul's whole argument against the circumcision of Gentiles rests on the impossibility of another baptism for those who die and rise again with Christ. His question to the Romans, for whom he had not laboured, 'Do you not know that all of us who have been baptized into Christ Jesus were baptized into his death? assumes that they must share this same belief.

2. IN THE EARLY CHURCH

Baptism in this sense is more than a rite or a series of rites. It is the gift of the Spirit, death and resurrection, salvation, conversion, communion. The order of parts is uncertain. Some receive the Spirit before baptism. Others have to wait until the apostles arrive. Some may be prepared and scrutinized before they are washed. Others received instruction after conversion, commitment, and baptism. In due course, as the Church grows, rules for admission will harden, but variations will still be seen as between Syria, Africa, and Rome, not only in the conditions for accepting candidates for baptism, but in the actual order of the rites themselves. No doubt in all churches catechumens, as they were called, were more carefully prepared, as the risks of premature reception into a persecuted Church became apparent.

[1] 11.26-30.   [2] Gal. 6.13-14.

Even so it is probable that baptized children were often instructed with them, and so were in a sense catechumens after baptism.

No doubt such children would be admitted to mysteries where other catechumens were excluded, and yet their baptism was less complete than that of their elder brethren. No one could be baptized again. The objection to rebaptism was so strong that the baptism of schismatics and even heretics (if in the threefold name) was eventually admitted against the opposition of those who baptized all converts because outside the Church there is no baptism, and no salvation. But in another sense each communicant was baptized anew in the eucharistic cup, and all looked for a baptism of blood, with Tertullian.[1] To die for Christ is to be baptized again, or, if unbaptized, to receive baptism.

Tertullian disapproved of infant baptisim and indeed of the baptism of the young:[2]

The baptism of the unmarried should be postponed, for in them a testing has been prepared alike for virgins through their maturity and for widows through their freedom from the duty of marriage, until they either marry or are hardened to the practice of continence. If any should understand the importance of baptism, they will be more afraid of its consequences than of its postponement; unimpaired faith is sure of salvation.

If he had been followed, the baptized would have become an inner circle, highly qualified by detailed instruction, much fasting, and an abundance of exorcisms, and baptism a reward for their strenuous exertions. The possibility of tension between S. Paul's doctrine of justification by faith and baptism is present in the very fact that baptism is a rite, but in the infant Church active tension is deferred by the baptism of infants and the baptism of blood. The first averted the assimilation of Christian to pagan mysteries, in spirit as well as in form. Christian initiates were not all perfected persons, reborn in a particular kind of religious experience. Some of them at least were beginners who knew nothing, not even what was going on, and yet they were committed by their sponsors to life, death, and resurrection in Christ. All were perfected in death,

[1] *De Baptismo*, c. 16.   [2] *Idem*, c. 18.

31

for martyrdom was the life of witness, of which execution was indeed the most satisfactory conclusion, but any Christian death can be a baptism.

The baptism of sick and dying catechumens was an exceptional measure for dealing with exceptional cases. Already in the middle of the third century exceptions to the exceptions, who recovered, created problems for the episcopal judgment.[1] In such cases a baptism of desire was always and is still admitted. Objections to rebaptism ruled out repetition of the central rite, but not of subordinate ceremonies. This paved the way, as we shall see, to a dangerously precise identification of stages in the rite with degrees of Christian baptism. It is significant that these problems were first raised in the case of adults, who might desire baptism in sickness. The extension of 'clinical baptism' to infants raised more serious problems, but these did not at once attract so much attention, probably because the infants concerned died. What can be called the theology of baptism in the early Church is based on the whole rite, water-baptism, the bishop's blessing, and first communion, and on the commitment implied therein. No one is yet concerned to isolate the effect of water on a frail infant in a brief transit between birth and death.

The point has been well brought out by M. Wladimir Weidlé, a Russian Orthodox historian of art, after summarizing a long debate between Roman Catholic and Protestant scholars about the symbols used in early Christian paintings found in the catacombs.[2] Most of these have some clear reference to baptism or the eucharist or to both. They are also signs of salvation. But all attempts to partition them between the two great Christian sacraments break down. Those that to some mean baptism, to others mean communion, or simply the gospel. 'What has a Christian to do with any salvation but that which through a sacrament made him a Christian ? . . . We can find the key to understand the early Church in general, and early Christian art in particular, only if we will refuse to divorce salvation and sacrament, even in thought.'

[1] See S. Cyprian, *Epistle* 69.   [2] In *The Baptism of Art*, 1949, pp. 16-17.

Our first description of baptism is in the *First Apology* of Justin Martyr, addressed to pagan readers not long before A.D. 140 or after 150. In such a pamphlet for the outside world omissions are to be expected, and little stress should be laid on these. What is important, is that Justin describes the baptismal eucharist[1] with some fullness before he speaks of the eucharist week by week[2] ('on the day which is called Sunday'). The baptismal eucharist is compared and contrasted, for pagan readers, with the initiations in the mysteries. The implication is that for Christians this is the greater mystery, while lesser mysteries are celebrated week by week and day by day.

Justin's description deserves a more detailed examination. It is included, as he explains:

Lest, by leaving it out, I should seem to be falsifying something in my description. Those who are convinced that what is said and taught by us is true, and so engage to live accordingly, are taught to fast and intercede with God for the forgiveness of their former trespasses, and we too pray and fast with them. Then we bring them to the place where water is, and by that way of regeneration, whereby we ourselves were new born, they too are born again.

We have learnt a reason from the Apostles for this. . . : Since we knew not our first birth, but were begotten by necessity . . . through the intercourse of our parents with one another, and were educated in unsatisfactory moral principles and evil cultural exercises, that we might not remain children of necessity, but become children of choice and knowledge, and that we might obtain forgiveness of those sins which we used to commit, a name is invoked in the water over him who chooses the new birth and repents.

This name that is spoken by him who performs the baptism is the name of the God and Father of all, and that alone, for no one can give a name to the ineffable God. . . . But also under the name of Jesus Christ, who was crucified under Pontius Pilate, and in the name of the Holy Ghost, who through the prophets proclaimed the things concerning this Jesus, he who is so illumined is baptized.

After so washing him who has made his convinced assent, we bring him to those who are called brethren, where they are gathered together to pray in common for themselves, and for the newly-enlightened and for all others everywhere. . . . When prayer is finished we salute one

---

[1] C. 61-6.   [2] C. 67.

another with a kiss. Then bread and a cup of wine and water mingled are brought to the president, and taking them he gives praise and glory to the Father of all through the name of his Son and of the Holy Spirit, and gives thanks at length because God has vouchsafed us these things. At the end of this the whole company approves the thanksgiving, saying, Amen, which in Hebrew means, let it be so. When the president has given thanks, and all present have assented, the deacons (as we call them) give to all who are there of the bread and water and wine over which this thanksgiving has been made, and carry portions away to the absent . . .

We do not receive them as ordinary food or drink, but as by the word of God, Jesus Christ our saviour was made flesh, and put on flesh and blood for our salvation, so also (as we are taught) the food that is blessed with thanksgiving by the word of prayer proceeding from him, that food whereby our flesh and blood is nourished, is the flesh and blood of Jesus who was made flesh.[1]

All things considered, this description of the baptismal euchar-ist is remarkably complete. We may take it for granted, though it is nowhere explicitly stated, that this is no ordinary occasion, but the annual commemoration of the death and resurrection of Christ, or of the descent of the Holy Ghost. By the time of Tertullian,[2] these were the two recognized times for baptism. A catechumenate of some duration is presupposed, with fasting in which all the brethren join. (This may be the first reference to the beginnings of a great fast before the Paschal feast.) Baptism in the threefold name is already accompanied by a confession of faith, probably in answer to questions, which seems to include 'suffered under Pontius Pilate'. It is compared to ritual lustrations before sacrifice, and to initiation into the mysteries, and completed, not by the bishop's blessing, which is not even mentioned in Justin's account, but by communion in the eucharistized gifts. These again are compared to the holy things of the Mithraic mysteries.[3]

Much that Justin Martyr omits may be found in the *Apostolic Tradition of Hippolytus*. It is now more than forty years since this

---

[1] Translated from Blunt's text, pp. 90-3, 97-100.

[2] *De Baptismo*, c. 19. Souter's 'Good Friday' is a misunderstanding.

[3] 'Bread and a cup of water are laid out in the initiations for one who is being made a *mystes*, with certain words, as you may know or learn.'

book was identified[1] as the common source of the so-called *Egyptian Church Order*, the *Testament of the Lord*, and other documents in a variety of languages, whose mutual relations had puzzled scholars for two hundred years. I see no reason to suppose that any alternative solution of this very difficult critical problem will now be propounded, but we are not yet out of the wood. In particular passages it is often very difficult to know which of the various texts, in Latin, Ethiopic, Arabic or Syriac, may be nearer the original meaning. And when we can be certain that we are dealing with the original text, and not with variations introduced in conformity with the custom of the place at the time when the adaptation was made, it is by no means certain that *Hippolytus* represents the authentic tradition of the church of Rome.

His editors have been at pains to insist on his conservatism, his stubborn resistance to the innovations in discipline introduced by Callistus, first as archdeacon to Pope Zephyrinus, and finally as Pope himself. Hippolytus, it is now believed, went into schism for conservative reasons and for many years claimed the see of Rome in opposition to Callistus and his successor Pontianus. It does not follow that he himself was innocent of all liturgical innovation. The English Nonjurors were conservative schismatics, and the Tractarians were a reactionary wing of the conservative High Church party in the Church of England, but it would be a grave mistake, though one that has been made, to reconstruct the opinions of Charles I and Archbishop Laud from those of Hickes and other Nonjurors, most especially in liturgical matters. The liturgical innovations of the Tractarians and their followers are with us to this day.

Nevertheless *Hippolytus* provides the best evidence that we can hope to have of baptismal ceremonies somewhere near the beginning of the third century, and on the points that matter for our present purpose, his text is reliable. His requirements for the catechumen may be extreme. His list of forbidden occupations

---

[1] By Dom R. H. Connolly in *The So-called Egyptian Church Order and Derived Documents*, Cambridge, 1916, and independently by E. Schwartz in 1910. (See *ibid.*, p. viii.)

includes one that we know figured in his controversies. He strongly disapproved of irregular unions between Christian ladies and their Christian slaves. These could not be legalized, where the law of inheritance was concerned, but were condoned, even favoured, by Zephyrinus and Callistus. However, even Hippolytus would baptize a concubine of a pagan master, 'if she have reared her children, and if she consort with him alone', but Christian masters, like Christian mistresses, must contract legal marriages or none. All concerned with the games, either as actors or spectators, are firmly rejected, but some hesitation is shown about schoolmasters, sculptors and painters. The two last may be able to avoid making idols. 'If a man teach children worldly knowledge, it is indeed well if he desist. But if he has no other trade by which to live, let him have forgiveness.' The perils of pagan literature cannot be avoided in school, but scholars cannot always turn their hands to other things.

Catechumens are to keep themselves apart from the faithful as yet and have their own prayers after their instructions. They have no part in the kiss of peace. When they are finally chosen as candidates for baptism their general behaviour is examined in the light of testimonials. If these are found satisfactory they are henceforth instructed in the gospel, and exorcized daily, at the final stage by the bishop himself. The meaning of 'scrutiny' in a later terminology is illuminated by the provision that a catechumen may be rejected, at least for the time being 'because he did not hear the word of instruction with faith. For the strange spirit remained with him.' This strange spirit might apparently escape the notice of lesser exorcists, yet be detected by the bishop himself. But this is one of the matters in which Hippolytus may be speaking as a sectarian, not as the guard of tradition.

The final exorcism takes place on the Saturday evening of the great week of vigil before the Paschal festival. The bishop, when he has finished exorcizing, is to breathe on the faces of the catechumens, and with his fingers seal (perhaps with oil) their foreheads, ears, and noses. The night is spent in vigil. They gather by the water, wherever it is, when the cock crows. The little children will first be undressed, and if they are too young to answer questions, their parents or relations must be ready to answer for them. The bishop has first prayed over the water, and made thanksgiving over two kinds of oil, the oil of thanksgiving and the oil of exorcism. This last is first used by the presbyter who demands from each catechumen, the babies first, that they renounce Satan, with all his works and service. The actual ritual of baptism is involved in some uncertainty on account of the ambiguity of references to 'the presbyter who stands by the water' and the deacon, who goes down with the catechumen. But clearly he does not baptize himself, but answers questions from presbyter or deacon. At each answer a hand is laid upon his head, and he is baptized. Immersion is clearly not intended to be total, except perhaps in the case of infants. But all are naked: no one may have any 'alien object', any charm or amulet.[1] The answers to questions, three in number, amount to a baptismal confession of faith:

In God the Father Almighty
In Jesus Christ, the Son of God,
Who was born by the Holy Spirit from the Virgin Mary,
Who was crucified in the days of Pontius Pilate,
And died,
And rose the third day living from the dead
And ascended into the heavens,
And sat down on the right hand of the Father,
And will come to judge the living and the dead.

In Holy Spirit in the Holy Church,
And the resurrection of the flesh.

The women are baptized last. In Syrian practice they were anointed by deaconesses, but of such beings Hippolytus knows nothing. He does however display some anxiety about the liturgical pretensions of widows, who may perhaps have baptized in the rival establishment.

After baptism all receive first the oil of thanksgiving from the attendant presbyter, and then, their clothes put on, a blessing from the bishop, who anoints them with oil on their heads and seals their foreheads. All then join in common prayer, the kiss of

[1] See Connolly, *Eg.C.O.*, p. 183 and n. 6.

peace, and the eucharistic thanksgiving. But in this special cups are blessed, of milk and honey, and of water. Communion is given to all from the three cups in succession, first water, then milk, then wine. From each cup each communicant drinks thrice 'in God the Father Almighty', 'And in the Lord Jesus Christ', 'And in Holy Spirit in the Holy Church'. Each time he answers 'Amen'. 'So shall it be done to each one.' This, I think, must mean every communicant in the baptismal eucharist. The milk and honey is interpreted as 'fulfilment of the promise made to the Fathers, wherein he said I will give you a land flowing with milk and honey; which Christ indeed gave, even his flesh, whereby those who believe are nourished like little children, making the bitterness of the heart sweet by . . . his word'. The water is 'an oblation for a sign of the laver, that the inner man also, which is psychic, may receive the same as the body'.

I do not find it easy to believe that all these rituals and explanations were ever common to the whole church of Rome. What is remarkable is the acceptance of this rite as a model in communities so far away as Syria, Transjordania, and Ethiopia. Hippolytus must have been in line with common Christian feeling when he elaborated in greater ritual detail the integration of the eucharist with baptism, and baptism with the eucharist. This is far more important than the position of the bishop's final blessing, in which he agrees with Tertullian and differs from the *Didascalia Apostolorum*. I cannot but think that the importance of this question has been exaggerated.

The bishop's prayer in *The Apostolic Tradition* runs thus:

O Lord God, who did count these worthy of deserving the forgiveness of sins by the laver of regeneration, make them worthy to be filled with thy Holy Spirit and send upon them Thy grace, that they may serve Thee according to Thy will; for to Thee is the glory. . . .

This precedes the anointing and sealing of the candidates after baptism, but in the *Didascalia Apostolorum*[1] a like anointing is prescribed before baptism:

[1] Ed. R. H. Connolly, Oxford, 1929, pp. 146-7. See also the Introduction, pp. xlviii-l, and the same editor's introduction to *The Liturgical Homilies of Narsai*, Cambridge, 1909, pp. xlii-xlix.

As of old the priests and kings were anointed in Israel, do thou in like manner, with the imposition of hand, anoint the head of those who receive baptism, whether of men or women; and afterwards—whether thou thyself baptize, or thou command the deacons and presbyters to baptize—let a deaconess . . . anoint the women. But let a man pronounce over them the invocation of the divine Names in the water.

Tertullian, whose commentary is upon an order like the one in *The Apostolic Tradition*, does indeed say

I do not mean to say that we obtain the Holy Spirit in the water, but having been cleansed in the water, we are being prepared under the angel for the Holy Spirit

and

The angel, the intermediary in baptism, 'makes straight the paths' for the Holy Spirit to come upon us, by the washing away of sins, obtained by faith that has been sealed in Father, Son and Holy Spirit.

Thereafter he writes of 'a hand . . . laid on us by way of blessing, summoning and inviting the Holy Spirit'. But I see no evidence that in his eyes the anointing 'with blessed unction according to the primitive practice by which priests were wont to be anointed with olive oil from a horn',[1] is more important than water-baptism. If in some of the Syrian writers the gift of the Holy Spirit is specially associated with the unction before baptism, in some of the same writers holy communion is to receive the Holy Ghost.[2]

The Holy Spirit is given before and after baptism, for none can confess Christ, except in the Holy Ghost. We may indeed read into Tertullian's comments some of the motives that led to a division of gifts between parts of the rite, but only in an embryonic form. His views on infant baptism were certainly his own. His objections to accepting any heretical baptisms were more common, but did not prevail in the end. His theology of the Holy Spirit before long led him into the Montanist sect, so that not much can be built on anything in his language that suggests a distinction between water and Spirit baptism. My own impression is that if

[1] *De Baptismo*, c. 6-8.
[2] E.g. *Narsai*, pp. 40-5, 58, and other examples cited in G. Dix, *The Shape of the Liturgy*, 1945, pp. 266-7.

there is one, it is between baptism as the dedication of a life, something that could be achieved by desire and death, and the rites as a whole, but not between baptism and anything corresponding to confirmation. Nevertheless, Tertullian's language is notoriously difficult. Few writers leave so many opportunities for reading between the lines.

Before we leave this part of the subject it might be well to notice a letter from Dionysius of Alexandria to Sixtus of Rome, preserved in Eusebius,[1] about an elderly Alexandrian Christian who developed doubts about his own baptism, received, as he then thought, in an heretical sect, but perhaps in some country church which had not arrived at Alexandrian standards of dignity in initiations. Dionysius had refused to rebaptize him,

Saying that his so long being in communion with us was sufficient for the purpose. For as he had heard the Giving of Thanks and joined in saying the Amen, and stood at the Table and stretched forth his hands to receive the holy Food and had taken it and partaken of the Body and Blood of our Lord Jesus Christ for a considerable period, I should not venture to put him back to the beginning once more.

The old man was still making difficulties, but the judgment of Dionysius was probably approved by Sixtus, certainly by Eusebius and others. The point is that the rites of initiation are a whole. The distinction of parts is a later development.

3. THE BEGINNING OF SEPARATIONS

This unity continued in practice as well as in theory, long after the possibility of a distinction of parts was recognized. This arose in part through the problem of heretical baptisms, in part through the recovery of those baptized in emergencies with something less than the complete ceremonies. On the question of heretical and schismatic baptisms there was much difference of opinion, never universally resolved.[2] Greek and Russian practice in this matter differed widely in the nineteenth century, nor does Roman

[1] *Eccles. Hist.*, VIII, c. 9.

[2] At Rome in S. Cyprian's time all schismatics recognized as baptized, whether in the Church or in the schism, could be reconciled in the same form. See his *Epistle* 74.

Catholic practice always seem to be in accordance with theory. But it is evident that if any irregular baptisms are admitted, they must be in some way confirmed, and for this the bishop's blessing provides the obvious form, especially in those rites where it comes at the end of the service. This principle once admitted, clinical baptisms will also be confirmed, with or without a catechumenate. Finally, in the Roman church, and in those Italian dioceses whose customs are taken from Rome, the bishops allowed baptisms in other churches besides cathedrals, baptisms conducted and completed by presbyters, on the condition that the final blessing was reserved to themselves.[1] This Roman custom spread with Roman books elsewhere in the West, but in the large dioceses beyond the Alps the effect was totally different. In Italy the cathedral baptisteries continued for many centuries to receive a multitude of infants, some for baptism, some only for confirmation, at every Paschal feast and every Pentecost.[2] But in the north the bishop's blessing became an addition to baptism, administered as the bishop travelled round his far-flung diocese, and only too often omitted altogether.

As important as the separation between baptism and confirmation is the development of private baptism in the Western churches from an expedient to something very like the regular rite. In this respect the difference between East and West is very marked and appears to have a theological as well as a social root. Tertullian, as we have seen, disapproved of infant baptism, and some in S. Cyprian's time had doubts about baptizing new-born infants before the eighth day. S. Cyprian's judgment was against such disdain for the infirmities of human flesh.[3] He clearly encouraged deacons to baptize in the home if this was demanded. Tertullian had allowed baptism by laymen, but not by women, in real emergencies.[4] In Africa this tradition continued, but when once the state of emergency was extended to the ordinary frailty of infants, whose chance of survival until Easter or Pentecost seemed at a

---

[1] See Innocent I to Decentius of Gubbio in M.P.L. 20, c. 554-5.
[2] This explains Dante's description of a scene in San Giovanni in *Inferno*, xix, vv. 16-21. See the commentators *ad loc.*
[3] *Epistle* 64.   [4] *De Baptismo*, c. 17.

given moment to be precarious, deaconesses, virgins, and widows were soon involved. In the fifth century the teaching of S. Augustine of Hippo, spreading from Africa into Italy and Gaul, laid a fresh emphasis, unknown to the East, on the risks of delay. The Council of Carthage in 418 denied any alleviation of suffering for the unhappy infant who died unbaptized.[1] Hell awaits all who are not saved.

This may have some roots in the local African religion,[2] certainly in the struggle between the Catholic church and the local schismatics, the Donatists, who denied all validity to Catholic baptisms, and threatened all their enemies, pagan and Christian, with a double dose of hell fire. S. Augustine's own misfortunes were perhaps more important. He was the child of a mixed marriage between a pagan father and a Catholic mother, who did not succeed in persuading his father to permit his baptism. He grew up unregenerate until his conversion, and wished others to be spared the same moral dangers. His voluminous works, far more comprehensive than any other Latin theological writings, did much to form the mind of the Middle Ages, and on this particular point they reinforced an already existing tendency to give a flexible interpretation to emergencies in the case of ailing infants, and so to reduce the number of children who are baptized at Easter and Pentecost.

Children were still brought to the Easter ceremonies. They were still exorcized and anointed. In many places, they were made catechumens. In some they were brought to the scrutinies which still continued on the appropriate Sundays, or, when displaced, on other days in Lent.[3] In Italian baptisteries, they were not only exorcized and anointed by priests, but confirmed by the bishop. In some north-Italian church, not a cathedral, efforts were still being made in the tenth and eleventh centuries to preserve the

[1] M.P.L. 56, c. 487.
[2] For the dedication of new-born infants to Caelestis, the Carthaginian Astarte, see Salvianus in M.P.L. 53, c. 154, and E. S. Bouchier, *Life and Letters in Roman Africa*, Oxford, 1913, p. 77.
[3] See *The Gelasian Sacramentary*, ed. H. A. Wilson, Oxford, 1894, pp. 45-60, and introduction, pp. xxxviii, lxvi-lxvii.

scrutinies at least in the latter part of Lent, and to adapt their ceremonies to the requirements of infant catechumens, most of whom, though not all, were already baptized.[1] In the north on the other hand, an opposite tendency is evident, to accumulate all the scrutinies and all the exorcisms, sometimes with other material derived from other preparatory rites, in the Easter and Whitsun ceremonies, where large numbers of small infants were successively scrutinized, exorcized, and anointed, but only a few were baptized.

The clearest statement of the position that I have been able to find is in the *York Manual*,[2] where it is laid down that children born within eight days of Easter or Pentecost ought to be 'reserved' for the solemn baptisms on the eves of these feasts, 'if they can be reserved suitably and without peril'. Such infants should receive the preliminary scrutinies and the other ceremonies relating to the making of a catechumen on an even earlier occasion, presumably at home, but be immersed only in the consecrated font. But those born 'at any other time of the year, on account of the mortal peril which often comes unexpectedly upon infants, should be baptized' without delay. The emphasis in mediaeval pastoral instruction on the duties of the laity in regard to baptism,[3] and still more in licences given to midwives[4] on their proper qualifications to baptize, most strongly suggests that in many parts of northern Europe what the Reformers called 'the Popish baptism of midwives' was the established custom at the time of the Reformation. It is hard to know how many of these baptized children were duly received at the Easter ceremonies or at some other time. Many clerics were undoubtedly confirmed before they were tonsured, confirmation being a necessary qualification for entry into the clerical class. It is certain that many more laymen and laywomen never received the bishop's blessing. This would seem

[1] See *North Italian Services of the XIth Century*, ed. C. Lambot, Henry Bradshaw Society, 1931.

[2] Edited by W. G. Henderson for the Surtees Society, 1875, p. 21.

[3] See John Myrc, *Instructions for Parish Priests*, ed. E. Peacock, EETS, 1902, pp. 18-20, and often elsewhere.

[4] Even after the Reformation. See Strype, *Annales*, Vol. I, pt. 2, pp. 242-3, in new ed. of 1824 (1567).

a serious obstacle to any theology of Christian initiation which would make this the climax of the rite.

In the East the whole approach to the problem was different. The integrity of Christian initiation was preserved, perhaps at the cost of too complete a separation between the rites of baptism and the common order of the Christian year. It was at least something that at every Easter and Whitsun common Christians in the West were reminded of their baptism. In the East they are reminded by the communion of infants. In the Eastern churches the demand for private baptisms, less insistent than in the West, was largely allayed by the provision of special prayers and blessings, on the eighth day in the home, and in the eighth week when the child is taken to church. These take the place of a catechumenate, and for a long time kept the parents patient until the child was strong enough to undergo the full baptismal ceremonies, including total immersion three times. Provision was always made for emergency baptisms, but lay baptism has often been discouraged, and never seems to have become the accepted practice.[1] Even under the stress of persecution parents will wait until their children can be baptized and confirmed by a priest.

No doubt in the fourth and fifth centuries they were baptized with adult catechumens at Easter and Pentecost or on other occasions when a baptismal eucharist might be celebrated, as on the Epiphany or on one of the great feasts of the Mother of God. S. Gregory Nazianzen advises that this should be postponed until they are three years old, and can be taught to make some answer to the baptismal questions.[2] It is likely enough that the prayers and blessings for them in their homes are as old as this. But before long infant baptism became possible at any time, in church or at home, but always with a liturgy of its own. This is modelled on the eucharist, with its own readings and chants, and a eucharistic prayer at the consecration of the holy oil and the holy water. The infant is stripped and anointed, exorcized, baptized and sealed with chrism blessed by a bishop, but the ordinary

[1] See H. Denzinger, *Ritus orientalium*, Wurzberg, 1864, t. i, pp. 41-4.
[2] *Oratio*, XL, § 28, in M.P.G., 36, c. 400.

minister of the whole sacrament, including this chrismation, corresponding to the Western confirmation, is the parish priest. Infants are communicated either immediately after baptism or on the first convenient occasion, and continue to make their communion in both kinds out of a spoon, until they reach the age of six or seven. After this they communicate seldom, for sin becomes their problem, but until then they are built in to the body of Christ as completely as possible.

Infant confirmation and communion were also practised in the West in the Middle Ages, but the weight of ecclesiastical authority was against confirmation by priests. The confirmation of children in arms however was not uncommon, and they were sometimes communicated, or given blessed wine to suck, long after lay communion in both kinds had normally ceased in the West.[1]

West and East in their understanding of baptism have both been influenced by particular pre-Christian backgrounds, but while the West seems to be haunted by the fear of demons surrounding dark and dangerous mysteries, the East, more especially the Greek East, is concerned with the new life, not only the life of the Church but the life of the city, the empire, the village, the family. Those initiated into the Christian Church must be filled with the Christ-Spirit, understood indeed in a quasi-physical sense. No doubt there are dangers in this, but it may be a better starting-point for a deeper idea of commitment than the fear of defilement, identified with original guilt.

We in the West have no need to deplore the separation of baptism from confirmation and first communion, the mercies shown to the frail in private baptism, or the opportunities of instruction afforded by a catechumenate before communion, so long as the unity of the whole rite is made plain. This could be done first of all by integrating adult baptisms and confirmations with the eucharist, in such a way that converts would normally be

[1] See A. A. Pellicia, *The Polity of the Christian Church*, Eng. trans., 1883, p. 19, and H. Holloway, *The Confirmation and communion of infants and young children*, 1901, pp. 17, 43, 61. Other instances of infant communion without confirmation can be collected from the rites of baptism at the end of the *York Manual* in Dr Henderson's edition.

baptized by the bishop, and received their first communion at his hands. In such a rite the common prayer of the Church, preparation for communion, and the eucharistic consecration, should follow immediately after the confirmation, as in the baptismal eucharist of the early Church. And at least sometimes the baptism of infants should take place in the Sunday eucharist, that they may be given to God in the sacrifice of Christ before the whole congregation.

In our present Western practice the effects of baptism overshadow its meaning.[1] On the one hand since the Reformation Catholics and Protestants have been engaged in controversies about the relation of baptism to spiritual regeneration. On the other Roman Catholics, Lutherans and Anglicans have comforted grieving parents with the thought that baptized infants, 'dying before they commit actual sin, are undoubtedly saved', in contrast with the unbaptized whose destiny is dubious. Anglicans have disputed among themselves about the gift of the Holy Ghost in baptism and confirmation. In these disputes the central meaning of baptism has often been forgotten, that it is the beginning of the Christian life, 'the interrogation of a good conscience toward God through the resurrection of Jesus Christ',[2] the risen life springing up in the soul. Whether this life is allowed to ripen will depend on the continuation of baptism, on the prayers of the Church, catechetical instruction, and the eucharistic food, but on any argument that allows any meaning to infant baptism, a beginning has been made.

[1] See G. W. Bromiley, *Baptism and the Anglican Reformers*, 1953, pp. 15-33.
[2] I Pet. 3.21.

OTHER INITIATIONS

I. MARRIAGE

IT has often been observed that in regard to marriage religion is more fertile in prohibition than in prescription. Forbidden degrees proliferate in every direction, but few religions impose penalties on bachelors and spinsters, and a religious regard for virginity is common to many civilizations. This arises partly out of exogamy. Every marriage is out of the family, and many out of the village and the tribe. Therefore in primitive societies to marry is often, though not always, to go after strange gods, or to receive a stranger into the house who may or may not be accepted by the gods of the family. Virgins who remain loyal to the hearth may therefore be specially honoured by the gods of hearth and home, as the Vestal Virgins were. Priests too may be wise to avoid strange women, especially if they serve a goddess. The priests of Cybele were compelled to be eunuchs. Marriage contracts are commonly modelled on treaties, and many marriage rituals symbolize the capture of the bride and her sacrifice to the gods of her new hearth.

It would appear to be an axiom that any law or religion with a wide range of geographical extension has an advantage over local custom in matrimonial matters; for this reason, that in high places, where standards are set for the lower classes, marriages are so often involved with matters of foreign trade. The first foundations of the Roman empire were laid in treaties binding allies to Rome through rights of trade and marriage, *commercium* and *connubium*. Where these rights prevailed the Roman law of marriage penetrated, long before the general concession of Roman citizenship, first to the Italians, and then after three more centuries to the empire's free inhabitants. The beginnings of Christian marriage are therefore conditioned by the forms of Roman law. No other traditions have more than a local importance. But Roman lawyers and Christian teachers had from the first an opposite emphasis. Roman law was concerned in the first place with the marriage contract and its fulfilment. With this the Christian Church had nothing directly to do. Even in the West in the Middle Ages, when the law of marriage had become the Church's own business, betrothals were generally conducted outside the church porch, in the view of the whole parish, as secular business. In early times no doubt pagan lawyers and pagan relations would claim a right to be concerned with the marriage settlements. These were signed and sealed at the bride's home. An exchange of presents, including a ring to the bride from the bridegroom, generally took place at the same time. The future partners clasped hands and kissed, and a date for the wedding was commonly fixed.

In the eyes of the Roman lawyers these espousals, followed by common life and a common bed, were sufficient to constitute a valid marriage. The marriage feast was less important. But in the eyes of the early Christians, who were not concerned with settlements, what mattered was the hallowing of sexual intercourse between the parties, the point of no return where the prohibited became the prescribed. For this the wedding feast was the appropriate moment, and the Christian love-feast provided a suitable setting, where the Church could entertain her poorer brides and bridegrooms.[1]

In the *Apostolic Tradition* of Hippolytus there is nothing about weddings, but a section about love-feasts, from which it appears that the bishop was accustomed to break a loaf beforehand, and to distribute portions, blessed to the faithful, exorcized to the catechumens. If the bishop did not come, a presbyter or a deacon might do the same.[2] This is not the eucharist, yet the practice points back to earlier days when communion in the bread and cup of the eucharistic thanksgiving was preceded or followed by a common meal for all the faithful. No doubt this breaking of bread took place before a Christian marriage in one of the two forms, as

[1] See Oscar Watkins, *Holy Matrimony*, 1895, pp. 78-88, and T. A. Lacey, *Marriage in Church and State*, ed. 1947, pp. 41-2.
[2] Pp. 45-8.

eucharist or as *agape*. Tertullian writes of the oblation, and also of the benediction of bride and bridegroom,[1] S. Ignatius of the bishop's sanction as given to weddings,[2] and Clement of Alexandria of an imposition of hands.[3] Where the bride was clad as a victim, veiled and garlanded as for a sacrifice to new gods, as common custom demanded, her garland must be removed at this point. Christian humility and Christian criticism of the ancient ritual demanded a further innovation. Her garlanding was postponed until the benediction. Then by a brilliant stroke of insight she and her husband were both crowned.[4] At Christian weddings in East and West both bride and groom were blessed, crowned, and enthroned on a bed, as kings and queens are anointed and crowned, to each other and to God.

Of this there are various forms. The primitive garland of olive-leaves or laurel, intertwined with flowers, is still in use in the Orthodox churches of Greece. In Russia metal crowns are covered with ikons. The Copts in Egypt anoint as well as crown. On the other hand they have no loving-cup as the Greeks and Russians have, nor do they dance in church. But they have a song:[5]

> Crowns unfading
> The Lord hath set
> Upon this bridegroom
> Of Jesus Christ.
>
> Shine, shine,
> O bridegroom
> And thy true bride
> Who shares thy happy state.
>
> Take the joy
> And the gift of God
> Which Christ our God
> Hath given to thee.

The Malabar Syrians no longer use a crown, but a gold chain with

---

[1] *Ad uxorem*, Bk. 2, c. 9.   [2] *Ep. to Polycarp.*
[3] *Paedogogos*, Bk. 3, c. 11.
[4] See DACL, x, c. 1890–1924, and v, fig. 4550, a small piece of glass in the British Museum of the third or fourth century.
[5] R. W. Woolley, *Coptic Offices*, 1930, p. 77.

a cross, held in the priest's hands in the form of a crown. Their poetry on this occasion is marked by 'a most apparent love of nature that is not characteristic of the people of Malabar'. Much also glorifies the union of Christ and his Church. One of the hymns translated by Bishop Brown is so close to the general theme of this book that it may well bear quotation at length:

> I am the Church, I am the Church and the Bride of the Most High,
> Blessed am I, whom he had betrothed to himself;
> I worship that Bridegroom who came down and betrothed himself to me,
> In the day when I was betrothed by him all creation was amazed at me,
> Who was poor and who suddenly became rich.
> Blessed am I because I have been exalted.
> He prepared for me a bridal chamber on high that I might rejoice with my friends;
> I entered in and sat down. Blessed am I who have confessed him.
> He took me away from the midst of idols
> And showed me hidden mysteries.
>
> . . . . . .
>
> Thanks be to Jesus who saved me.
> Blessed am I, for I have been made worthy.
> He clothed me with the armour of the Spirit,
> Through the water of baptism,
> And he placed on my finger as a ring,
> His holy body and blood.
> The Bridegroom is like unto the sun,
> And the Bride is like unto the daylight,
> And the feast is like unto a tree putting forth sweet fragrance.
>
> . . . . .
>
> I searched for him among the multitudes.
> I heard the voice of one speaking from the crowd,
> 'The Lover of this Holy woman has been crucified on the Tree on Golgotha'
> I wept bitterly and followed him to Zion;
> When I entered the city they told me,
> 'The Jews have placed him in a sepulchre'.
> I wept bitterly leaning my head against the Tree;
> An angel answered me and said, 'Weep not! He is risen from the tomb'.
> I heard his voice and rejoiced;
> My face shone and I was full of joy,
> I held him and embraced him,

He answered me lovingly and said:
'Peace be unto thee, O worthy woman,
Who hast been betrothed to me on the Cross,
I ascend to the Father and I send to thee the Holy Spirit.'[1]

The rites ring the changes on the great theme of the fifth chapter of Ephesians:[2]

Husbands, love your wives, even as Christ also loved the church, and gave himself up for it; that he might sanctify it, having cleansed it by the washing of water with the word, that he might present the church to himself a glorious church, not having spot or wrinkle or any such thing; but that it should be holy and without blemish. . . . For this cause shall a man leave his father and mother, and shall cleave to his wife; and the twain shall become one flesh. This mystery is great: but I speak in regard of Christ and of the church.

In the English rites of the Middle Ages the betrothed pair were brought into the church and blessed at the altar steps. They stood in the presbytery, between the choir and the altar, on the south side, with the bride on the right, while mass of the Holy Trinity was said or sung, in some rites with a proper preface and other propers of its own. In the Sarum and in the Hereford orders the bride and bridegroom lay prostrate before the altar during the prayer of consecration from the sanctus to the end of the Lord's Prayer, while a canopy or pall was held over them. After the fraction they knelt to receive 'the sacramental benediction' under the pall, and in front of the altar. Before the communion they rose again, and the bridegroom received from the priest the kiss of peace. He kissed the bride and both made their immediate preparation for communion. According to the Sarum rite, if they did not communicate, they received blessed bread and wine at the end of mass. In all the rites their bed was solemnly blessed.

This nuptial benediction under the pall was not given to second marriages, at least in the case of widows, as in the Eastern rites second and subsequent marriages were not normally crowned. However by the end of the Middle Ages it had become customary

[1] L. W. Brown, *The Indian Christians of St Thomas*, Cambridge, 1956, pp. 256-9.
[2] Vv. 25-32.

to use the greater part of the prayer of blessing on such occasions, without the pall, omitting only what was considered proper to 'the sacramental benediction', in Sarum:

O God, who hast consecrated the state of matrimony to such an excellent mystery, that in it is signified the sacramental and nuptial union between Christ and his church.

At the Reformation all distinction between first and second marriages disappeared, and the pall vanished. The whole nuptial blessing was given, with little alteration, before the celebration of Holy Communion. This remained an integral part of the Solemnization of Matrimony until the Civil War. The same nuptial blessing is now given at the end of the Anglican marriage service. In the *Roman Missal* printed in Milan in 1474[1] the sacramental blessing is in the same place as in the mediaeval English rites, but in the Pian Missal it is earlier, after the Lord's Prayer, and before the fraction. Nothing is written of the pall, which seems to have been disappearing gradually in the Roman Catholic communion since the Reformation.

Something may usefully be said of a difference between East and West about the sacramental significance of the nuptial benediction. In the Eastern churches the sacrament of marriage is the crowning. Other marriages may be recognized as lawful by church and state, but only crowned first marriages are properly sacramental. Something like this seems to be implicit in some of the Western liturgical forms, but in the end the influence of the canonists prevailed to this extent, that every marriage between Christians allowed by the Church was allowed as a sacrament, of which the parties themselves are ministers. In the settled doctrine of the later canonists any contract whose purpose is the present beginning or continuation of married life is a lawful, and between Christians a sacramental marriage, although an unconsummated marriage may be subsequently annulled. An engagement to marry is an impediment to marriage with another, though one that can be removed.[2] It seems likely that in the Middle Ages a great

[1] Ed. H. Lippe for HBS, 1907, Vol. II, p. 321.
[2] Lacey, pp. 41-4, 106-7.

number of espousals and marriages were not performed in the churchyard or in the church, and many had no blessing from a priest. His presence was not reckoned necessary to the regularity of a marriage before the Council of Trent, and this was not immediately received in Roman Catholic Europe. In the *Pontifical of Archbishop Egbert*[1] of York, an eighth-century work printed from a tenth-century manuscript, there are a number of benedictions evidently intended to sanctify marriages already in being, including blessings for the bed and the ring, but no sacramental benediction for use at mass. The full nuptial mass was more common in the West than in the East, where the length of the liturgy precluded its combination with marriage rites and family festivities, but in the West the nuptial blessing was a luxury for the rich, whereas in the East all first marriages were crowned in church.

In the East bishops and councils were concerned with the conditions for a nuptial blessing, and with the admission of married people to communion or penance. The marriage as such was the concern of the lawyers. In parts of the East, in the Moslem world and in Russia, the lawyers, or at least the judges, were ecclesiastics, administering the personal law of the Christian people in lands where the secular authorities were incompetent or unwilling, but this law was Byzantine, the *Nomocanon*, a revision of Roman law under Christian influence. Divorce was allowed, but only for grave causes. Divorce by consent had been eliminated, and the conditions changed to the wife's advantage. Divorced persons might remarry, and their marriages were blessed, but like widows and widowers, they were not crowned, and they might have to undergo a period of penance.[2]

In the West divorce was impossible, but private marriages were common in all classes, hard to prove, and in practice easily annulled. The deserted wife whose husband had entered on a more prosperous union would find it very difficult to recover him, if she

---

[1] Edited by W. Greenwell for the Surtees Society, 1853, pp. 125-6, 132.

[2] Lacey, pp. 108-11; Watkins, *op. cit.*, pp. 346-62. See my own *Byzantine Patriarchate*, 1947, pp. 23, 141.

could not produce a witness for her account of the contract, which he might honestly remember in another sense, since he now believed that he had been entrapped. This was really a greater scandal than the irregular unions of the great, whose marriages were not concealed, and could not be repudiated. Not until the joint action of church and state against secret marriages[1] made marriage in church the common custom in all Western lands except Scotland (where mediaeval manners lingered), was there any widespread demand for relief from broken marriages, and this may be partly due to the declining hold of Christian standards in the same period. Nevertheless the increasing divergence between the marriage laws of the state and the Church may eventually drive us to consider again the ancient and Eastern Christian distinction between valid marriage and the sacramental benediction.

At any rate, a church wedding in the fullest sense, with a celebration of the eucharist, ought to be a feast of the local church. Under modern conditions it is often impossible for the bride and bridegroom to entertain all their friends at the bride's home, and so they resort to a restaurant. This may be a more convenient place in all respects than the church rooms, but this need not prevent the wedding breakfast from becoming a church feast. The fullest possible hallowing of the beginnings of married life may make a great difference to young people in a world where success in marriage is no longer taken for granted, and a certain apprehension of failure often hangs over homes in the first years. In this context the teaching of some of the early Christians that the bond of the bridal dedication is of such a kind that it should survive death has a new relevance. This is considered, in Christian writings, chiefly in relation to second and third marriages, which were for a long time reluctantly condoned, and in special cases condemned, not only in the East but also in the West.[2] An impression is sometimes left by these discussions that all marriage is a

---

[1] E.g. in Lord Hardwicke's Marriage Act of 1753. See Lacey, pp. 166-8.
[2] Much material is conveniently collected in E. Martene, *De antiquis ecclesiae ritibus*, ed. Venice, 1783, t. ii, pp. 121-2.

concession to the flesh, and once is enough, but I do not think that this is the whole story.

Objections to the remarriage of widows and widowers, and rules against it where priests and deacons were concerned, were already well established in the time of Tertullian.[1] They still persist in the Eastern churches, where married men and women have played a larger part[2] in forming the Church's mind on such issues than in the West where all ecclesiastical leaders were celibates in the Middle Ages. In the East monks and bishops have often been widowers. There is therefore no necessary connection between objections to second marriages and that extravagant emphasis on celibacy which reached its first peak at the end of the third century, and afterwards had more persistence in the West than in the East. We should rather look for the source of such objections in the ideals of Christian married couples, who would not allow that death could divide them, while admitting at other moments that some allowances might have to be made in a fallen world, not only for death, but for the tragic consequences of unfaithfulness. This provides an explanation for the inconsistency, by later Western standards, of those early Christian and Eastern Christian moralists, who not only discouraged second and third marriages, but also forbade priests and deacons to continue with their wives if they proved unfaithful,[3] and yet allowed the forsaken wife or husband the possibility of other espousals, in contrast with the Western insistence that death, but death alone, dissolvse the bond.

2. CORONATION

This is not the place for a full discussion of the long and elaborate ceremonies of our own royal coronation, but their place

---

[1] See *Ad uxorem*, Bk. i, c. 7.

[2] E.g. a law of the Emperor Leo VI (886-912) in M.P.G., 107, c. 604, maintains with examples from animal behaviour that permanent widowhood is in accordance with the proper dignity of human nature. That the emperor himself failed to keep this law does not detract from the significance of his argument.

[3] See Watkins, *op. cit.*, pp. 227-9, 296-301, and the Byzantine canonists in M.P.G., 137, c. 1216-17, on the eighth canon of Neo-Caesarea.

in the order of the eucharist is relevant to the theme of this book. This is not, as many might suppose, a survival from mediaeval practice, but an innovation made at the coronation of William and Mary, after the Revolution of 1689. The kings of England before the Reformation were crowned before a high mass; and the first three Stuarts followed this precedent, making a conservative adaptation of the ancient rites to the new condition of religious affairs. But James II, being a Roman Catholic, was crowned without a eucharist. William and Mary, in striking contrast, were crowned within the eucharist. At their coronation everything except the recognition and 'the first oblation' was deferred until after the creed and sermon. The oath, the anointings, the acceptance and oblation of the sword, all the investitures, the coronation, inthronization, and homage, led up to the 'second oblation' of bread and wine and of a mark of gold, at the offertory of the eucharist.

This 'second oblation' was indeed part of the mediaeval rite. Archbishop Laud, when he translated and edited this for Charles I in 1626, adapted the proper secret to serve as an offertory prayer:

Bless, O Lord, we beseech thee these thy gifts, and sanctify them unto this holy use, that by them we may be made partakers of the Body and Bloud of thine onely begotten Son Jesus Christ: And thy Servant Charles may be fedd unto everlasting life of soule and body, and enabled to the discharge of this great place and Office whereunto thou hast called him. Of thy great goodnesse grant this O Lord for the honour of Jesus Christ his sake, our onely Mediatour and Advocate. Amen.[1]

Since 1689 this has become the final action of the coronation, though the prayer may be followed by a blessing (in 1953 of the Duke of Edinburgh). The homage of the peers, that follows the inthronization, is solemnly concluded by the oblation of the sovereign in the eucharistic action.

This is the more significant if we consider the original meaning of inthronization. Under the throne is the stone of Scone. The

[1] *The Coronation of King Charles the First*, ed. Chr. Wordsworth, H.B.S., 1892, p. 50.

legends relating to the stone are relatively recent, but the stone itself is certainly ancient, and sufficiently sacred in the eyes of some Scots and Picts to make Scone, an otherwise insignificant town, the proper place for the enthronement of a king of Scots, as at Kingston-on-Thames another stone was at one time the proper throne of the West Saxon kings. The stone of Scone, like the hill of Tara in Ireland, was an altar or trysting-place between tribes and their ancestors, long before its mythology was loosely linked with the Old Testament by attributing to Pharaoh's daughter its transport from Egypt to Compostella. The route is right, Spain, Ireland, Scotland, the pathway of pioneers of religion and culture round to the north and west of these islands. The anointing and enthronement of Christian kings have a remote background in religions where the king is the anointed priest standing at or even on the altar to be the mediator between God and man, the image of God to man and of man to God. In our own rite he is still enthroned on a pyramidal theatre, which not so long ago was built up to the level of the high altar, and still stands between the altar and the congregation, but as soon as the homage is over, he or she goes straight from the throne and from the homage of his brethren to present on their behalf bread and wine, the elements of the Christian eucharist, at God's board. The king is a priest only in the sense in which all Christians are priests. He fulfils at that moment the characteristic liturgy of Christian laymen and Christian women, offering for them and with them our common oblation in the sacrifice of Christ.

The actual coronation, in the narrower sense of the term, is only one part of an elaborate ceremony of investiture with regalia between the unction and the inthronization. In most of the mediaeval rites the sceptre and rod come at the climax of this, after the crown and after the ring. They did so still at Charles I's coronation. The rod, the *baculum*, is a more primitive and elementary symbol of kingship than the crown, diadem, or helm. It is the wizard's wand, while the crown belongs to the *imperator*, the leader in war. This came into western coronations from the Roman empire, which was always more like a secular dictatorship than a sacred monarchy. Nevertheless the Roman power was so great that the imperial crown has become the most familiar royal emblem, and we now speak of the whole rite as the coronation. The present order, sceptre, rod, crown, is in the *Pontifical of Egbert*. It is not simply a modern invention.

This raises the difficult question of the sources for the reconstruction of 1689. Writers at the end of Queen Victoria's reign, notably Mr J. Wickham Legg, regarded the mutilated coronation order used by Archbishop Sancroft for the coronation of James II in 1685, and the order of 1689, as two successive steps in the disintegration of the ancient rite. I have a better opinion of both. It is clear that Archbishop Sancroft played a considerable part in the composition of his own order.[1] In 1689 he refused to crown the new sovereigns, or to take the oath of allegiance in the lifetime of James II, but he provided the Bishop of London, Henry Compton, with a sheaf of papers relating to previous coronations,[2] and many (perhaps too many) of the prayers composed by him in 1685 were used again with little or no alteration. The great innovation, the change in the structure of the rite, is generally attributed to Bishop Compton himself. Mr Legg[3] wrote:

It is likely that one of the things that Dr Henry Compton, the bishop of London, had in mind in the revision of the coronation order was the insertion of the coronation into the celebration of the Lord's Supper, so that the sovereign could no longer avoid making his communion at the hands of the prelate who had crowned him.

And again:

It is in this place that the consecration of a bishop is inserted in the book of common prayer, and a reminiscence of this may have been present in Dr Compton's mind, and determined the place.

Compton was no liturgist, but a man of affairs. Therefore, it is held, his agreement with some ancient precedents 'may have been

---

[1] *Three Coronation Orders* HBS, 1900, preface by J. Wickham Legg, p. xviii, with reference to Bodleian Tanner MSS., Vol. 31, f. 86.

[2] E. Carpenter, *The Protestant Bishop*, 1956, p. 151.

[3] *Loc. cit.*, pp. xx-xxi.

due more to accident than to learning'.[1] But in a tense political situation unprecedented innovations require a kind of daring which Compton did not possess. It is as difficult to imagine a liturgist of lesser rank persuading him to take an unprecedented course.

It is true that the most obvious precedent, the office for the benediction of a king in the *Pontifical of Egbert*, which contains much of the mediaeval matter in something like the 1689 order, and between the Gospel and the offertory, was not published (by Dom Martène of S. Maur) until 1702.[2] But it was probably known to the experts earlier, and some consultations between Roman Catholic and Anglican liturgists before the coronation of James II are not at all unlikely, though they would not be publicized on either side. In any case there are other precedents for coronations within the liturgy, those of Byzantine emperors, Russian czars, and German kings crowned at Aachen. In an age when interest in liturgical antiquities was steadily growing, and much correspondence between scholars crossed confessional and national frontiers, I see no reason to attribute a brilliant dramatic success to a shot in the dark.

In the long run however sources are less important than results. Since 1689 our present order has made a powerful impression, not only on successive generations of the nobility and gentry, but on some of the more sensitive individuals called to occupy the throne. The results were not always happy. George III wrote gravely to Pitt:[3]

A sense of religious as well as political duty has made me, from the moment I mounted the throne, consider the Oath that the wisdom of our forefathers has enjoined the Kings of this realm to take at their Coronation, and enforced by the obligation of instantly following it in the course of the ceremony with taking the sacrament, as so binding a religious obligation on me to maintain the fundamental maxims on

[1] *Ibid.*, pp. xxix-xxx.
[2] In *De antiquis ecclesiae ritibus*, t. ii, pp. 214-15, in ed. 1783.
[3] February 1, 1801, in Lord Stanhope, *Life of Pitt*, Vol. III, 1862, Appendix, pp. xxviii-ix; cf. Vol. II, appendix, pp. xxiv-xxv: 'measures to prevent which my family was invited to mount the throne . . . in preference to the House of Savoy' (February 6, 1795).

which our Constitution is based, . . . that those who hold employments in the State must be obliged . . . to receive the Holy Communion agreeably to the rites of the Church of England.

Queen Victoria took a less denominational view of her position, but certainly thought much of her duty to the Protestant succession in the matter of 'putting down ritualism'. Nevertheless it would be a mistake to imagine that either George III or Victoria thought of their spiritual obligations always in this negative sense. Both contributed something to the pattern of princely duty which we have come to associate with the crown through the enduring devotion of George V and George VI.

The decline of the political power of the crown has brought an increase not so much in its spiritual influence as in its potency as a symbol. Other reasons besides the seriousness of the Prince Consort contributed to the higher moral tone of the Victorian age as compared with the Regency, and the Edwardian era really began in the 'nineties. But the good Queen and the Prince of Wales did serve as symbols. Edward VII after his coronation was a different kind of symbol from the rebel prince of the former reign.

The sacramental character of the coronation has probably become clearer as it has become dissociated from all recollection of the sacramental test. No doubt if we had a king who was not in communion with the Church of England either the mediaeval arrangement would be revived, and the king crowned in the Abbey before a celebration, or the whole ceremony would be abandoned.

The second is the more probable alternative, since no coronation has been held elsewhere in Europe since King Haakon of Norway was crowned in 1906.[1] The coronation is a survival, not of absolute monarchy, which has left no trace on the rites or the rubrics, but of an hierarchical relationship between estates of the realm, a contract between king and people. That is why it can be used to symbolize the complex relationships between parts of the British Commonwealth. But the form would fall to pieces without

[1] See R. W. Woolley, *Coronation Rites*, Cambridge, 1915, p. 156.

relation, not simply to religion in general, but to a particular religion and a particular act of religious dedication.

One improvement might be desired if the coronation continues. In the rite prepared for King Charles I the rubric[1] implies (or so it seems to me) that the Archbishop proceeded directly from his blessing of the king after the offertory to the eucharistic consecration. Here at this moment, when the symbolic significance of the offertory is most clearly revealed as the king himself, like Melchizedek of old, brings forth bread and wine for his people to be united with the sacrifice of Christ, the preface ('Lift up your hearts') would seem to be the right response. Prayer for the church has already been made in the Litany, and confession could be made before the offertory.

From one point of view the nuptial benediction and the coronation, like baptisms at Easter and Whitsun and other blessings in the eucharist, are part of the eucharistic mystery itself. From another the eucharist is the repeatable and repeated part of the baptismal action, baptism, confirmation, communion. This whole action is better represented by the coronation of the queen or the consecration of a bishop than by the Sunday and daily eucharist, a detached part of the baptismal rite added to an abbreviated version of the synagogue service or church meeting. This signifies little to the uninitiated, whereas in the coronation the whole rite, especially the eucharist, came alive and spoke to those who knew nothing about it. This might happen more often if the Church was prepared to consecrate persons in the eucharist, not only to be ordained ministers, but like the queen, to perform secular liturgies. For this there are other precedents besides the coronation and the nuptial benediction, in the many forms of religious profession accepted by the Church in ancient and modern times. The widows and virgins of the early Church were certainly not ordained ministers, nor were they cloistered monks or nuns. They followed a variety of occupations, but kept themselves free from ties that they might be used by the Spirit and the Church as the need arose. As marriage was also blessed, this did not involve an antithesis

[1] Ed. Chr. Wordsworth, p. 51 and note.

between the Church and the family. 'Only, as the Lord hath distributed to each man, as God hath called each, so let him walk.'[1]

But there is no necessary connection between solemn dedication and the choice of celibacy or marriage. In a church whose ordained ministers are free to marry or not, many parish clergy would wish to consecrate organists and scoutmasters, and to give a blessing to young men about to join the armed services, to young women qualified to be nurses, in the public liturgy of the Church. The offertory between the *synaxis* or church meeting and the eucharistic thanksgiving is the best place for an elaborate rite of dedication such as the coronation or the consecration of a bishop, and for adult baptism and confirmation, but other dedications may be better done in other places, some, like the nuptial benediction, at the time of communion. If week by week the children of the Church were solemnly blessed in the eucharist, the whole people of God would be recalled to their dedication to the service of Christ in the act of communion.

[1] I Cor. 7.17.

CHAPTER FOUR

THE CHRISTIAN PROSPHORA

THE eucharist is first of all an action, the breaking of bread, the cup of blessing. The bread and cup are taken, blessed with thanksgiving, divided, and consumed. Other actions may be added, baptism, ordination, marriage, the church meeting, the common meal before or after or even between the bread and the cup, but these compose what Dom Gregory Dix called 'the four-action shape'.[1] On two points his understanding of the shape is open to criticism. The second is not important, that the fraction is of the bread, not of the cup, and may be more conveniently regarded as one of the practical preliminaries to communion.[2] The first is more important than may appear at first sight.

I. THE TAKING

Dom Gregory Dix explicitly identified the 'taking' with the offertory: 'bread and wine are "taken" and placed on the table together.'[3] The doubt relates to the order. In many existing rites at any rate one of the sacramental elements, if not both, is placed on the table long before they are taken into the liturgical action. In a Roman 'low mass', for instance, the host is on the paten when it is first brought in at the beginning, and in the Dominican rite the chalice is mixed and filled long before the eucharistic action is begun. In Dom Gregory Dix's interpretation of the *Apostolic Tradition*[4] of Hippolytus all the offerings of bread and wine and of food and flowers of every kind were made before and in the eucharistic thanksgiving. But according to the *First Apology* of Justin Martyr,[5] the collections in money and kind were taken after the communion, and this would fit the evidence of *The*

---

[1] *The Shape of the Liturgy*, pp. 48, 78.
[2] For the history of mystical interpretations of the fraction, see J. A. Jungmann, *The Mass of the Roman Rite*, Eng. trans., New York, 1955, Vol. II, pp. 298-311.
[3] *Shape*, p. 48.   [4] Pp. 10-11, 53-5.   [5] C. 67.

Apostolic Tradition in so far as any inferences can be drawn from the position of the prayers of offering, some of them after the eucharistic thanksgiving, others in another place. The point is important only in view of the meaning and effect which could be attached to the offerings of particular communicants in association with intercessions for a particular end.[1] I see no reason to suppose that the collection of loaves and phials of wine before the eucharistic thanksgiving was ever a universal custom. The baking of a common loaf or loaves from flour or grain provided by the faithful at the end of the last meeting is just as likely to be primitive.[2] This would be more practical than the collection of loaves of various shapes and sizes, and of phials containing many varieties of wine. In one or another form it has now become the general custom, and the eloquent symbolism of many grains gathered into one loaf was familiar to the early Church, for instance in the *Didache*:[3]

As this that is broken was sown upon the hills and gathered and made one, so let thy Church be gathered from the ends of the earth into thy kingdom.

And in Irenaeus:[4]

As out of dry wheat a lump or a loaf cannot be made without water, so we being many could not be made one in Christ Jesus without the heavenly water.

I do not press these allusions as proof that the common loaf was baked in the primitive Church, but I see no evidence that it was not. Where it is, the collection of materials for the eucharist is only remotely connected with the action, which begins when they are taken as matter for sacrifice.

At this point in the action gestures are older, and speak louder, than words. A procession of the prepared elements from the

---

[1] See *infra*, pp. 65, 90.
[2] See Dix, *Shape*, pp. 118-23, but cf. F. Cabrol on 'offertoire' in DACL, xii, c. 1947-62, G. J. Booth, *The Offertory Rite in the Ordo Romanus Primus*, Washington, 1948, A. Clark in *Ephemerides liturgicae* 64, Rome, 1950, pp. 309-44, *ibid.*, 67, 1953, pp. 242-7 (on Booth). I owe these references to the Rev. R. P. Symonds.
[3] C. 9.   [4] *Against Heresies*, Bk. iii, c. 18.

diakonicon, a separate room close to the entrance of the church, or from a credence table or altar of prothesis to the Lord's table, the altar proper, is a natural development from the simple introduction of bread, wine, and water described by Justin Martyr.[1]

Provision is made for a diakonicon to receive the people's oblations in the *Testamentum Domini*, one of the church orders modelled on the *Apostolic Tradition*.[2] (This is generally assigned to the middle of the fourth century, and to somewhere in Asia Minor.) Buildings of this description have been identified in some of the ruined churches of Transjordania,[3] dating from the fourth, fifth, and sixth centuries. A sacrarium of the same kind is attested in Gaul in the sixth century, in an entertaining story told by Gregory of Tours[4] of a widow who, in memory of her late husband, was accustomed to offer a bottle of the best wine, but did not always make her communion. Warned by an apparition, she did so, and tasted vinegar so sour that she thought her teeth would come out. She then accused the subdeacon of stealing from the sacrarium. This story is important as showing that not every reference to offerers in relation to the sacramental elements need refer to an offertory procession, or to any other kind of collection in or immediately before the sacrificial action.

The widow regarded herself as an offerer, bringing her oblation as her forefathers had done to the shrines of other divinities. She expected the priest to perfect it for the forgiveness of her husband's sins and for the rest of his unquiet spirit. The Church everywhere recognized the special claims of offerers to intercessions, more especially in the eucharist, but tradition might support the subdeacon if he held, as perhaps he did, that the oblations in the sacrarium could be applied to any worthy purpose, including the relief of his own necessities. (That he took the wine does not seem to me certain; perhaps he spoilt it by leaving the bottle open.) In the view that prevailed in the Eastern, and sometimes in Western

[1] *First Apology*, c. 67, after the account of baptism.
[2] Eng. trans., *The Testament of the Lord*, ed. J. Cooper and A. J. Macleane, Edinburgh, 1902, c. 19, p. 62.
[3] J. W. Crowfoot, *Early Churches in Palestine*, 1941, pp. 56-7.
[4] *Liber de gloria confessorum*, c. 65, in M.P.L., 71, c. 875-6.

churches, the bread and cup are the Church's offerings, made out of the oblations of her members, but before they ever enter the Church, symbols of the mystical body of Christ and of his Body and Blood.

The procession from the diaconikon to the altar is first described in detail by Theodore of Mopsuestia in *Catecheses* given in Cilicia, probably before 392.[1] In his church the procession took place in silence, but his comparison of the deacons to angels recalls the *cherubikon*, or angelic hymn. Of this the version in the Liturgy of S. James,[2] familiar to English readers through the hymn 'Let all mortal flesh keep silence . . .', is still used in the Byzantine rite on Easter Eve:

Stand in fear and trembling, and think of nothing earthly, for the King of Kings, Christ our God, comes to be sacrificed and given for food to the faithful. Before him go the choirs of angels with all authority and power, the many-eyed cherubim and the six-winged seraphim covering their faces and crying Alleluia.

This hymn may have been influenced by Theodore's interpretation of the eucharistic rite as a drama, in which the Lord is buried on the altar to rise again at the invocation of the Holy Ghost in the climax of the eucharistic thanksgiving.[3] On the other hand in some form it may be older than his time, although not yet in use at Mopsuestia. Something like it is described, less than a century after, in the *Ecclesiastical Hierarchy* of Dionysius the Areopagite,[4] a Syrian work intended to represent the liturgical uses of the apostolic Church. On the other hand in the *Apostolic Constitutions*, also from Syria, and also a reconstruction of primitive church order, compiled before the time of Theodore, there is no sign of any elaborate ceremony at the 'great entrance'.

---

[1] *Homélies Catéchétiques*, ed. R. Tonneau and R. Devréesse, French translation and facsimiles of the Syriac, Rome, 1949, pp. 463-4, 495-511. There is an English translation by A. Mingana in *Woodbrooke Studies*, V, Cambridge, 1932.

[2] F. E. Brightman, *Liturgies Eastern and Western*, Oxford, 1896, pp. 41-2. I do not commend the version in *The English Hymnal* as a translation.

[3] Developed in the fifth and sixth homilies, *Mops.*, pp. 461-605.

[4] M.P.G. 4, c 425, 436.

The *cherubikon* made its way into the Byzantine liturgy, according to Cedrenus,[1] in the ninth year of the Emperor Justin II (573-4). The ex-Patriarch Eutychius, deposed some time before in 565, preached a sermon against it, possibly after his restoration to office in 577, on the ground that 'the bread of the prothesis' and 'the cup that has just been filled' were called 'the King of glory' before 'the high-priestly invocation and hallowing'.[2] This cannot refer precisely to the present Byzantine version of the *cherubikon*.[3] The present form may be a result of this protest:

Let us who mystically represent the cherubim, singing the hymn trisagion to the life-giving Trinity, cast aside all earthly cares, that we may receive the King of all invisibly attended by the angelic hosts, alleluia, alleluia.

This is cautious ('mystically', 'invisibly') and caution is all that Eutychius wants, some reserve until the mystery is perfected.

The salutation of the unconsecrated elements as an image of Christ was not confined to the Byzantine empire or Syria. We find it over the border in Persian Mesopotamia,[4] and also, like the sacrarium, at Tours. Gregory of Tours, in telling another good story,[5] has to say how

The time came for offering the sacrifice, and the deacon, taking the tower (*acceptaque turre*) in which the mystery of the Lord's Body was laid, began to bear it to the door, and entered the temple to place it on the altar, but it slipped from his hand and was carried through the air, and so came of itself to the very altar, nor could the hands of that deacon ever catch it. . . .

The expression, 'the mystery of the Lord's Body' tells the same tale as the *Cherubikon*, of the veneration of the prepared elements, gathered together to represent Christ and his body the Church.[6]

---

[1] *Compendium of the Histories*, M.P.G., 121, c. 748.

[2] M.P.G., 86b, c. 2400-2.

[3] But cf. the corresponding hymn in the liturgy of the pre-sanctified gifts, where the reserved eucharist is addressed as 'The King of Glory' as 'The mystical sacrifice, all accomplished, is ushered in'.

[4] See *Narsai*, p. 3.

[5] *De Gloria Martyrum*, M.P.L., 71, c. 781; cf. 'Germanus of Paris' in M.P.L., 72, c. 92-3.

[6] But it has been argued that the reference is to the *sancta*, consecrated at a previous eucharist, here and in 'Germanus'. See W. H. Freestone, *The Sacrament Reserved*, Alcuin Club, 1917, pp. 77-8.

This cannot be due to any recent Eastern influence, for the sixth century was a bad time for communications between Gaul and the East. As Dr Norman Baynes has shown, Gregory's ideas about Byzantium were vague in the extreme.[1] It is rather a case of parallel inferences from parallel practices. In Gaul[2] as in the East the sacramental elements were generally prepared in a diakonicon or sacrarium, and by rites of prothesis fashioned for their purpose. They became symbols in the baking and making.

After a time the preparation of the elements moved from the diakonicon to the church itself, either to an altar or table of prothesis, as in the Byzantine and Armenian rites, or to the altar before the readings, as in the rites of the Copts, Ethiopians, and Jacobites. In the West this was the more common.[3] In several French cathedrals and in Westminster Abbey the chalice was still made in the sacristy at the end of the Middle Ages, and in the rite of Salisbury on a day of general communion the hosts were prepared in the *vestibulum chori*.[4] But on ordinary days, when very little was needed, it was enough to prepare the sacramental elements at the altar, either at the beginning of mass, as in the Sarum rite, or between the epistle and the gospel as at a Dominican high mass today,[5] or finally in the Roman place between *oremus*, all that is left of the ancient general intercession (except on Good Friday), and the immediate preparation for the eucharistic thanksgiving.

In the Roman mass the prothesis is directly involved in the taking of the elements to be blessed. The chalice is mixed when the host has already been taken for the first time. No Western rites of prothesis flowered into the wealth of symbolic detail characteristic of the protheses of the East, where the figure of the Lamb of God is prepared for the sacrifice, and remembrance is made of the saints, of the faithful departed, of other churches, and of the

---

[1] In *Byzantine Studies and other Essays*, 1955, pp. 313-15.

[2] See the long study by J. W. Legg in *Ecclesiological Essays*, 1905, pp. 91-178.

[3] See J. W. Legg, *loc. cit.*, especially the tables on pp. 164-78.

[4] *Salisbury Processions and Ceremonies*, ed. Chr. Wordsworth, Cambridge, 1901, p. 88.

[5] At a low mass they are prepared at the beginning.

offerers, in the preparation of particular portions.[1] But in the West as well as in the East the union of water and wine is a symbol of the incarnation:

Grant us through the mystery of this water and wine to be partners in His divinity, who condescended to be a partaker in our humanity.

Already when this prayer is made the host has been called 'this immaculate victim', and the host and chalice together are offered a moment later as 'This sacrifice prepared for Thy holy name'. These prayers in the ordinary of the Roman mass are not in the oldest texts,[2] but some of the so-called secret prayers in the sacramentaries have the same symbolism, and in the oldest text of what at least seems to be the canon of the Roman mass, quoted in the *De Sacramentis* of S. Ambrose, the first prayer after the *sanctus* is:

Fac nobis . . . hanc oblationem, ascriptam, ratam, rationabilem: quod figura est corporis et sanguinis Domini nostri Jesu Christi.

Make this oblation approved, ratified, reasonable, acceptable, seeing that it is the figure of the Body and Blood of our Lord . . .[3]

In the account of the baptismal eucharist in the *Apostolic Tradition* of Hippolytus,[4] we are told that the bishop

shall eucharistize the bread into the *exemplum* (which the Greeks call the antitype) of the flesh of Christ: and the cup mixed with wine for the antitype (which the Greeks call the similitude) of the blood that was shed for all who believed in Him.

Here indeed the antitypes are the fruit of the thanksgiving. In the liturgy of S. Basil it is the antitypes that are offered immediately before the invocation of the Holy Ghost that he may bless and hallow the bread and cup, and show them to be the Body and Blood of Christ. The two ideas do not exclude one another. In the *Catecheses* of Theodore of Mopsuestia,[5] who as we have seen hailed the eucharistic elements as symbols at the great entrance:

[1] See E. S. Drower, *Water into Wine*, especially pp. 48-60, 123-96, and Jungmann, ii, pp. 31-47.

[2] Jungmann, ii, pp. 41-3.

[3] Book iv, c. 5, trans. T. Thompson, ed. J. H. Srawley, 1919.

[4] C. xxiii, p. 40; cf. *supra*, p. 34.   [5] *Mops.*, p. 583.

We are constrained to participate in these mysteries because by the means of this sort of figures (types), in signs too lofty for speech, we believe ourselves to possess already the realities themselves, that we have received indeed in the communion of the mysteries the first-fruits of the Holy Ghost, believing also that in baptism we take hold of the new birth, but in communion we receive in faith the food and subsistence of life.

The roots of this language go deep. The great value of Lady Drower's book, *Water into Wine* (despite some obscurity in detail), lies in her rare insight into what may be called psychological connections between the later developments of Christian liturgical practice in the East and the old agricultural religions. No doubt many Christians, and many more pagans, have regarded sacrifice as a gift, to propitiate an angry god, but a gift theory of sacrifice presupposes private property, and where property belongs to the group, it also belongs to the tribal god. Whatever Jews and Christians may sometimes say, the number of pagans who really believe that the gods require sacrifices to feed themselves is certainly limited. The provision of large numbers of victims on great occasions ought rather to be interpreted as emphasis. Guests are invited to a banquet, not because they cannot otherwise feed themselves, but to make a point of doing them worship, in the old English sense. Sacrifice is first of all an acted prayer, a commemoration before God (or the gods) of human needs in a figure which is also a gift. When the prayer is heard, the present received, the gift becomes a sign, and omens and auspices are sought in the posture of the victim and in the condition of the sacred flesh.

Where the sacrifice of Christ is understood in these terms as the perfect offering of the second Adam, the representative man who in his death and resurrection is revealed as the great high priest and the saving victim, the eucharist is seen as the commemoration of Christ in figure by his command, and by his promise the communion of his Body and Blood. But in another aspect the bread and cup are first-fruits of creation and symbols of the Church. This idea is as old as Justin Martyr, who wrote in his *Dialogue with Trypho*:[1]

[1] C. 117, trans. A. Lukyn Williams, 1930, pp. 241-2.

Now that prayers and thanksgivings, when made by worthy people, are the only perfect and acceptable sacrifices to God, I also myself affirm. For these alone were Christians taught to make, even at the remembrance of their food, both dry and liquid, in which also the suffering which the Son of God has suffered for their sake is brought to mind.

So also in Irenaeus:[1]

We offer His own to Him, fittingly proclaiming the communion and union of flesh and spirit. For as bread from the earth, receiving the invocation of God, is no longer common bread, but eucharist, consisting of two things, earthly and heavenly: so also our bodies, receiving the eucharist, are no longer corruptible, having the hope of resurrection.

2. THE THANKSGIVING

The eucharistic thanksgiving is a prayer of offering because it is the prayer of blessing, the grace before heavenly meat. In a wider sense all who say grace offer to God his own of his own. In the eucharist, as in other graces, the aspect of offering is often, but not always,[2] expressed in words. The communion could be given without any words at all. But the thanksgiving, the blessing, is a matter of words about ineffable things. In the earliest times this had no set form, but probably followed a pattern, based on the three themes of the baptismal interrogation and confession. In his description of the baptismal eucharist,[3] and in his brief appendix on Sunday worship[4] Justin Martyr insists that:

Over all things that we offer we praise the maker of all things through his Son Jesus Christ and through the Holy Spirit.

The first two themes are expanded in the *Dialogue with Trypho*:[5]

Jesus Christ our Lord ordered us to do this in remembrance of the suffering which He suffered on behalf of those who are being purged in soul from all iniquity, in order that we should at the same time give

[1] *Adversus haereses*, Bk. iv, c. 31.

[2] For the exceptions see A. Linton, *Twenty-five Consecration Prayers*, 1921, p. 23, and for an example, p. 123, the Mozarabic mass for the Epiphany, translated from the *Liber Sacramentorum*, ed. D. M. Ferotin, Paris, 1912, pp. 88-91.

[3] *Supra*, pp. 33-4.   [4] *First Apology*, c. 67.

[5] C. 41, trans. A. L. Williams, pp. 81-2.

thanks to God for having created the world with all that is in it for man's sake, and also for having set us free from the evil in which we had (hitherto) been, and for having destroyed the powers and authorities with a complete destruction by means of Him who became liable to suffering according to His will.

We may also safely suppose that his account of the institution of the eucharist has a liturgical source. But for the third theme we are obliged to turn to the thanksgiving proposed on the occasion of the consecration of a new bishop in the *Apostolic Tradition*.[1]

This has been the centre of liturgical discussions for the last forty years, since it was first identified as the earliest extant example of a prayer of consecration. Certain cautions are not always observed. The first is that the context is an ordination. It is nowhere said or implied that this is the general eucharistic prayer, although only one phrase—'making eucharist to Thee because Thou hast found us worthy to stand before Thee and minister as priests to Thee'—seems specially appropriate to the occasion. The second is that Hippolytus was bishop of a schismatic group, and had theological ideas which in his time were 'advanced', although his line of approach was on the whole in what proved to be the orthodox direction. A number of specific resemblances to the other writings of Hippolytus in the prayer, were listed some twenty years ago by Dom R. H. Connolly,[2] who was himself largely responsible for establishing his authorship of the *Apostolic Tradition*. These lie entirely in the central Christological section, where the specific interests of Hippolytus lay. The end and the beginning are more likely to be common form.

First the deacons bring the oblations to the bishop, and he with all the presbyters lays hands upon them. This is the offertory, the taking. The thanksgiving begins with the universal invitation and response.

℣. The Lord be with you   ℟. And with thy spirit
℣. Lift up your hearts   ℟. We have them with the Lord
℣. Let us give thanks unto the Lord   ℟. Meet and right

[1] C. iv, pp. 7-8.
[2] In an article on 'The eucharistic prayer of Hippolytus' in *The Journal of Theological Studies*, xxxix (1938), pp. 350-69.

'Meet and right' in the later liturgies is the opening for a commemoration of creation. None follows in the text, but it does not seem to me certain that none was intended. Two other eucharistic prayers are known in fragmentary form[1] which pass from 'meet and right' almost directly to the commemoration of Christ, but they do thank the Father first:

It is meet and right that we should here and in all places give thanks unto Thee, O holy Lord Almighty God: nor is there any other through whom we can have access unto Thee. . . .

The other is very similar. So far as I know they are the only extant prayers of consecration except those derived from the *Apostolic Tradition* that do not include the sanctus,[2] and they may have had it at a later stage. Hippolytus may have had it between 'meet and right' and the commemoration of redemption, or as it has been argued,[3] at the end. We may conclude that the sanctus is almost universal, and with it some commemoration of creation, since the sanctus has: 'Heaven and earth are full of thy glory.' The commemoration of redemption by Christ is universal, in manifold forms. The difficult questions arise in relation to the commemoration of 'The Holy Spirit in the Holy Church and the resurrection of the flesh'.

The end of the prayer of Hippolytus in the Latin and Ethiopian versions[4] is:

And we pray Thee that Thou wouldest send Thy Holy Spirit upon the oblation of Thy Holy Church, and grant a gathering into one to all Thy holy ones who receive for the fulfilment of the Holy Spirit unto the confirmation of their faith in truth; that we may laud and glorify Thee through Thy Son Jesus Christ, through Whom to Thee be glory and honour, to the Father and the Son with the Holy Spirit in Thy Holy Church now and to ages of ages.

[1] See H. F. Stewart, *The Development of Christian Worship*, 1953, pp. 98-101, and Dix, *Shape*, pp. 539-41. These prayers, probably from north Italy, are quoted from orthodox rites by an Arian controversialist of the fifth century.

[2] See Jungmann, ii, p. 132.

[3] By E. C. Ratcliff in two articles on 'The Sanctus and the pattern of the early anaphora' in *The Journal of Ecclesiastical History*, Vol. I, 1950, pp. 29-36, 125-34.

[4] *Ap. Trad.*, pp. 75-6. The differences are insignificant.

The Syriac *Testament of the Lord* omits the actual invocation of the Holy Spirit upon the oblation, but all three Persons have been invoked earlier in the same prayer, which in this version has been expanded to three times its original length.[1] If the Latin or the Ethiopian text is accepted as authentic, it does not follow that the Holy Spirit was at any time everywhere invoked, or even remembered by name. The arguments depend on 'considerations outside the scope of textual discussion', as Dom Gregory Dix allowed.[2]

Two prayers in the *Didache*[3] may be relevant. The first, which has been already quoted,[4] is more likely to belong to the *agape* than to the eucharist, but the second might well be eucharistic. Both have a threefold form, beginning with praise to the Father through the Son, and concluding with prayer for the Church, in the second prayer thus:

Remember, O Lord, Thy Church to deliver her from all evil, and perfect her in Thy love, and gather her from the four winds that has been sanctified for the kingdom which Thou hast prepared for her.

This may be another instance of commemoration of 'Holy Spirit in Holy Church and the resurrection of the flesh' in the thanksgiving. The Roman canon and many of the eucharistic prayers in the Gallican and Mozarabic missals superseded by the Roman mass in the Middle Ages have no invocation of the Holy Ghost to descend and bless the oblations, but they end in prayer for the unity of the Church and for her fulfilment with the Holy Spirit in the heavenly places, as in the Roman prayer *supplices te rogamus*:

We most humbly beseech Thee, Almighty God, command these things to be carried by the hands of Thy holy angel to Thy altar on high, in the sight of Thy divine majesty, that as many of us who by participation at this altar shall receive the most sacred Body and Blood of Thy Son, may be filled with all heavenly benediction and grace through the same Christ our Lord. Amen.

This Amen may well have been the original end of the canon. The

---

[1] Chapter 23, pp. 71-5 in the edition of Cooper and Macleane. The invocation is at the top of p. 74.

[2] In *Ap. Trad.*, note on p. 75.

[3] In Chapters 9 and 10.   [4] *Supra*, p. 64.

memorial of the dead which now follows is certainly a later insertion, but the memorial of the saints in the *nobis quoque peccatoribus* continues the same theme of union in heaven.

The real difference between East and West in the eucharistic thanksgiving is not so much concerned with the form of consecration, whether by the words of our Lord in the institution of the sacrament or by the invocation of the Holy Ghost, as with the matter of the sacrifice. In the old Mozarabic and Gallican masses, used in Spain and France in the early Middle Ages, the place of the offering and of the invocation, sometimes of the Holy Ghost, sometimes of the Holy Trinity, to bless the oblation, varies from day to day and from feast to feast. In some there are no words expressing oblation, for the action is enough. The fixed elements are the introductory versicles, 'Lift up your hearts . . . it is meet and right so to do', the sanctus, commemorating creation, the narrative of the institution, and the Lord's Prayer.

This scheme is common to East and West, although in many instances some of the elements of the thanksgiving have been transposed, so that for instance the commemoration of redemption through Christ, or prayer for the Church, may begin before the sanctus, but the original pattern seems to me sufficiently plain. The whole prayer is addressed to the Father. . . . Very soon, if not from the very beginning,[1] a commemoration of creation is introduced somewhere near the opening, now invariably including the sanctus, 'Heaven and earth are fully of thy glory'. What in the Mozarabic missals is called the *post-sanctus* follows, leading to the commemoration of the institution of the eucharist and of the passion, resurrection, and ascension of Christ. The prayer concludes with petition for the Church, and especially for the communicants, sometimes but not always including a prayer that the Holy Ghost may descend in blessing upon the elements, or that they may be accepted in the heavenly places. This prayer *post-pridie* or *post-mysterium* in the Gallican and Mozarabic missals varies greatly in length and considerably in content. I see no

[1] For the commemoration of creation in Jewish graces see *Tractate Berakoth*, vi, i, Eng. trans. by A. Lukyn Williams, 1921, p. 43.

reason to believe that it was ever considered to be the form of consecration in the sense in which the invocation of the Holy Ghost was, and now is, in the East. On the other hand many of its forms are inconsistent with the idea that the consecration is already completed by the recitation of our Lord's words in the narrative of the institution. An easily accessible example is in the Missal of Reichenau,[1] and there are many more:

We beseech the glory of our Lord and our eternal God, praying that thou wouldest bless this sacrifice with Thy benediction, and besprinkle it with the dew of Thy Holy Spirit, that to all who receive it may be a legitimate eucharist; through Jesus Christ.

Some however say much less:

Bless, O Lord, this host that has been offered for the honour of thy name, and sanctify the mind and purify the will of all who receive therefrom.[2]

This and a short invariable ending are in this mass all that intervenes between the narrative of the institution and the Amen of the canon.

3. CONSECRATION/SACRIFICE

The developing difference between East and West is concerned with something else. Some tension between Constantinople and Rome in liturgical matters may be observed in the correspondence of Pope Gregory the Great, who had to defend himself from the charge of making Byzantinizing innovations in the Roman mass.[3] The conflicts of East and West in the eighth and ninth centuries also turned to some extent upon liturgical issues in regard to such matters as ikons. But no one made any complaint about the prayer of consecration, so far as I can discover, until the thirteenth century,[4] when the schism was already an accomplished fact. By that time however for two hundred years there had been a

---

[1] Neale and Forbes, p. 4, Linton, p. 115.   [2] *Lib. Sacr.*, pp. 632-3.
[3] His reply in M.P.L., 77, c. 955-8.
[4] Manuel, the Great Rhetor of Constantinople, in his reply to Friar Francis (*c.* 1240) in M.P.G. 140, c. 481, seems to be the earliest critic of the Roman canon.

continuous conflict on the subject of the eucharistic bread.[1] This seems to be petty and even frivolous, but conceals something very important. If the bread and cup are an image of Christ in the prothesis and the great entrance, they must be the right image. The wine must be mixed, in commemoration of the two natures,[2] or by an older symbolism, of the water of baptism,[3] and the bread must be real bread, not a collection of wafers, for it is this image, these antitypes that are offered, that they may become the Body and Blood of Christ. These are also offered in the Roman mass, before the consecration, but also after the narrative of the institution. Is this the same offering, or not the same?

This question was asked and answered by Pope Innocent III, who cannot be accused of orientalizing sympathies, some time before the controversy between East and West, so far as the eucharist is concerned, shifted from leavened and unleavened bread to the form of consecration. Before his own accession to the Papacy (1198) he wrote in his *De sacro altaris mysterio*:[4]

It seems therefore that in respect of the order of the eucharistic consecration the section beginning: *qui pridie quam pateretur*, ought to have been placed at the end of the canon, since in it the consecration is consummated, but since this would have impeded the order of the historical narration, because what was done in the middle, would have been put at the end, the arranger of the canon, that he might preserve the order of the history, compelled as it were by a certain necessity, placed this section in the very heart of the canon, . . . in the middle of it, so that what follows is understood as going before.

So also the author of the *glossa ordinaria* on the *Decretum* of Gratian, a commentary written a few years later, round about 1215,[5] wrote of the *supplices te rogamus*:

[1] For the beginnings see my *Byzantine Patriarchate*, pp. 157, 166-7, and refs.
[2] Jungmann, ii, pp. 39-41.
[3] *Mops.*, p. 483: 'It is suitable that the chalice should be diluted with water, since the bread has water in it. There cannot be bread without a mixture of water. And as for the baptismal birth we make use of this type, we use it also in the sacrament of food and in the cup.'
[4] M.P.L. 217, c. 888. See the comment in M. De La Taille, *Mysterium Fidei*, Eng. trans., 1950, Vol. II, p. 424, n. 1.
[5] On *Pars tertia, de consecratione*, dist. 2, quoted *ibid.*, p. 419.

It seems that this prayer is superfluous, because it is said after the words by virtue of which the Body of Christ is made (*conficitur*), and hence the prayer about what has been done is superfluous. I reply: not only does Scripture not attend to such strict time limits, but the priest too, as he cannot say many things at once, so speaks as if time stood still, and as if those things still had to be done which at the beginning of his speech had not yet been done.

But within a few years the great elevation, with the ringing of bells at the moment of consecration, had spread all over Western Christendom. In the eyes at least of popular devotion, time no longer stood still, and the Body and Blood of Christ were first made and then sacrificed, not only in heaven but on earth. To reject this as a repetition of the one sacrifice meant either to reject the sacrifice, or to deny the real presence.

But the great Byzantine commentator, Nicholas Cabasilas, had another and a better answer, when he wrote in the middle of the fourteenth century in his *Explication of the Divine Liturgy*:[1]

The bread, from the simple unsacrificed bread that it was, is changed into a sacrificed object. It is changed from simple bread that has not been sacrificed into the Body of Christ which has been really slain. . . .

If it was the bread that, remaining altogether bread, became the sacrificed object, it would be the bread that received the immolation, and then it would be the immolation of the bread that would be the sacrifice. But the change bears upon two things, on the fact of being unsacrificed, and on the bread. The unsacrificed object, the bread, has become the sacrificed object, the simple bread has become the Body of Christ. It follows that this immolation, considered not in the bread but in the Body of Christ . . . is called and really is the sacrifice, not of the bread but of the Lamb of God. . . . The reality in which this transformation is produced must indeed be one and the same thing, a unique Body, and unique also is the immolation of the Body.

It was on the basis of this theology of the essential nature of sacrifice that Cabasilas affirmed that in the Roman mass, whose text he had carefully studied, the true equivalent of the Byzantine epiclesis was the prayer *supplices te rogamus*, wherein the offerings are borne by the angel's hand to the altar in heaven.[2] He denied

[1] M.P.G., 155, c. 440-1, French trans. by S. Salaville, *Explication de la divine liturgie*, Paris, 1943, pp. 181-3, with notes, pp. 183-7.
[2] *Ibid.*, c. 428-33 and pp. 148-78.

the Western theory of consecration, but not the sufficiency of the Roman canon.

In this he was the heir of a great tradition. The same theory of consecration is presented in a less developed form, which may be more acceptable to the Western reader, in the *Catecheses* of Theodore of Mopsuestia.[1]

All the priests of the new covenant offer the same sacrifice continually in all places and at all times: because the sacrifice that was offered for us is unique, the sacrifice of Christ our Lord, who for us accepted death and by the oblation of this sacrifice achieved perfection for us, as the blessed Paul says: *By one offering he has made perfect for ever them that are being sanctified.* So we in every place and at all times continually make the *anamnesis* of this same sacrifice, because every time we eat this bread and drink this cup, we make *anamnesis* of the death of our Lord, until he come. . . . It is himself, now still, who by the means of these types is immolated.

Cabasilas came after controversies that led him to lay more emphasis than Theodore on the difference between the ikon of Christ in the bread and cup of the prothesis and the great entrance, and Christ himself 'lying behind the appearances'[2] at the time of communion. He knew, and did not contradict, the Western doctrine of transubstantiation. But in his insistence on a single sacrifice he was consciously protesting against the Latin practice of making 'a great number of oblations of the Lord's Body',[3] and against Latin theories of sacrifice that are constructed to justify this. It is significant that his French translator treats his interpretation of the Roman canon with great respect, and finds his central thesis on the object of sacrifice repeated and amplified in the writings of modern French theologians, Bouesse, De La Taille, and Masure. De La Taille[4] writes:

Once we admit as legitimate the principle of ceremonial expansion through the successive parts of the Liturgy, we have a reasonable explanation of petitioning for the consecration after the enunciation of the sacrifice has been made, and this has been preceded by the commemoration of the Supper.

[1] *Mops.*, pp. 495-7.   [2] M.P.G., 150, c. 440 D.
[3] *Ibid.*   [4] *Mysterium Fidei*, ii, pp. 423-5.

79

But if this principle is to be conveyed to the faithful, it would seem to involve either some qualification in the doctrine of a 'moment of consecration', and an adjustment of the ceremonial accordingly, or a rearrangement of the canon so that the moment stands at the climax.

The idea of a moment of consecration is one that must inevitably arise from the reflection that the consecration of the eucharist cannot be conceived as a gradual process, an infiltration of divine substance,[1] but as so often happened with other theological problems, such reflections came late. In the Roman canon prayer for consecration of the elements 'that they may become the Body and Blood of Christ' came before the narrative of the institution, which therefore became in the Roman tradition, the moment of consecration, but the prayers after the narrative were not therefore interpreted as referring to another and different oblation than the oblations in the prayers before it. But in the East the invocation of the Holy Ghost to bless the elements came not only after the narrative of the institution, but after the offering of the antitypes, at the very climax. Prayer for the communicants follows, and has been expanded in most of the liturgies into a general intercession for the whole Church. It is indeed probable, as we have said, that the invocation of the Holy Ghost at this point grew out of prayer for the unity of the Church through her communion in the Body and Blood of Christ. But when in a popular manual[2] it is asserted that by the Eastern Fathers the epiclesis was

defined as being the moment of consecration, but—and this is of importance—not defined as such in relation to the Oblation,

some reserves are necessary.

It is indeed true that the object of the unique sacrifice is Christ himself. In this East and West are in complete agreement. But after the Iconoclast controversy a clearer distinction was made in the East between the antitypes that are offered and the gifts that are received. The Iconoclasts,[3] who objected to pictorial

---

[1] See E. L. Mascall, *Corpus Christi*, 1953, pp. 73-4.   [2] Linton, p. 28.
[3] At their own 'oecumenical council' held in Constantinople in 754, quoted in Darwell Stone, *A History of the Doctrine of the Holy Eucharist*, 1909, Vol. I, pp. 148-9.

representations of Christ, insisted that the bread and cup of the eucharist were his only ikon, that 'No other form was chosen by Him, and no other figure can be an image of His incarnation'. These figures, 'The God-given image of His flesh, the divine bread, together with the cup of the life-giving blood from His side' were 'filled with the Holy Ghost' at the consecration of the eucharist, 'the priest mediating by making the offering in the transference of that which is common so as to be holy'. The orthodox reply[1] was to insist that 'before the consecration they were called antitypes but after the consecration they are called, and are, and are believed to be properly the body and blood of Christ'. The image of the body cannot be the divine body itself.

It has been pointed out[2] that

Iconoclasts and Iconophiles started from a different conception of the image. With the former it was in some way identical with the person represented, with the latter there existed only a relation between them.

This might be more precisely put by saying that to the Iconoclasts the bread of the prothesis and the great entrance represented the Body of Christ not because of any resemblance, but by his command. Their orthodox opponents did not deny this, but in defending images of another kind they became chary of using the word in regard to the eucharist, most of all in regard to the consecrated elements which in earlier days had often been called types. Henceforth the veneration given to the bread and cup at the great entrance is *proskynesis*, 'relative regard', of the kind that can be given to an ikon. *Latreia*, divine worship, is reserved for the gifts after the consecration and in the communion, and this is addressed to Christ himself in them, not to the elements as symbols in any sense. This may be why no cult of the reserved sacrament has ever arisen in the East, except in the liturgy of the pre-sanctified gifts, where the elements reserved from a previous celebration are carried in at the great entrance for the communion of the ministers on the

---

[1] At the Second Council of Nicaea, quoted *ibid.*
[2] By P. Alexander, *The Patriarch Nicephorus of Constantinople*, Oxford, 1958, p. 209.

days when the liturgy is not completed. In the East the real presence is always closely associated with the communion.

4. THE DECLINE IN FREQUENT COMMUNION

The decline of frequent communion is common to East and West in the fourth and fifth centuries and continued through the whole of the Middle Ages. In the days of persecution, as in the *Apostolic Tradition*, it was assumed that a faithful Christian would wish to communicate daily. Provision was[1] made for communion at home from a eucharist kept safely, where no unbeliever might find it 'nor a mouse or other animal, and that none of it at all fall and be lost'. The details in the various versions are not easy to follow, but the very fact that these provisions were still included testifies to the practice in other parts of Christendom than Rome. It was understood at least in Arabia and Egypt. Tertullian is a witness to it in Africa.[2] I am inclined to think that the bread was probably dipped in the consecrated cup, like the *fermentum* which at a later time the Pope sent to the presbyters of the titular churches in Rome. This was placed in a cup at home, and wine added with a blessing. So I should explain

For having blessed the cup in the Name of God thou didst receive it as the antitype of the Blood of Christ.[3]

At first sight this looks like lay consecration, but if this had ever been permissible the point would have been made in later controversies. On the other hand the principle of consecration by contact[4] of wine and water added to the cup was known in much later times. With this some prayer of blessing might very naturally be associated. The eucharist was taken before any meal. In Christian families we may imagine that the first meal of the day would be both eucharist and *agape*. It is significant that Hippolytus has very little to say of the Sunday eucharist, which may have been regarded in his community chiefly as the occasion for the distribution of eucharists to be carried home. He does urge the faithful to

[1] Pp. 58-9.
[2] *De oratione*, c. 9, *Ad uxorem*, Bk. ii, c. 5, cf. Connolly, *Eg.C.O.*, p. 81, n. 1.
[3] *Ap. Trad.*, p. 59.   [4] See Jungmann, ii, pp. 315-16.

be zealous in attending opportunities of instruction and the church meeting 'where the Spirit abounds'.

But as soon as the Church emerges from persecution a new attitude to the eucharist appears. For this the responsibility is often laid at the door of the authors of Catechetical lectures, especially S. Cyril of Jerusalem and Theodore of Mopsuestia, whom we have so often quoted before. But before we blame them for laying such heavy stress upon 'fear and trembling' as the proper attitude before communion, we ought to consider their pastoral problem. We know little about Mopsuestia except what may be gathered from incidental allusions in Theodore's own writings, but a good deal about Jerusalem. We know that S. Cyril and his successors presided over Paschal ceremonies in a new baptistery and in the *Martyrium*, both adjoining the *Anastasis*, the rotunda round the Holy Sepulchre. At Pentecost on the other hand the eucharist was in the *Coenaculum*, the upper church on Mount Sion, the traditional site of the descent of the Holy Ghost. On both occasions throngs of pilgrims must have been present in the years of excitement that followed the first establishment of the Holy Places in and about Jerusalem. A stern hand was needed to keep the devout congregation under any sort of control.

No doubt Jerusalem was exceptionally difficult, but the bishops there had some advantages in that they could promote the extension of church building with great speed, and regardless of cost. Elsewhere the building of churches failed to keep pace with the influx of converts. Derelict temples were seldom suitable for the purpose. Rome, the old capital, now deserted by the government, was fortunate in possessing a large supply of unwanted public buildings, the Roman basilicas, which were swiftly and easily adapted. But in many places crowded congregations must have found it hard to preserve recollection and reverence as they approached the mysteries.

The distribution of eucharists under these conditions was impracticable in the greater churches. Those who copied the provisions of the *Apostolic Tradition* seem to have been small country communities, where eucharists might still be carried to lonely houses and hermits' cells. We know from some lives of the saints that some hermits and stylites continued to receive eucharists in their places of refuge at a much later period, even after the practice was forbidden by the canons of the council in Trullo (691-2).[1] But the distribution of eucharists probably ceased in the cities at a much earlier period, as celebrations conducted by presbyters in what may already be called parish churches took the place of family communions conducted by the head of the household.

As small groups of Christians give place to crowded churches the practical problems attending communion must have become much more difficult. Some complaints of S. John Chrysostom[2] against 'shameless and impudent persons' who did not make their communion at Antioch may have been directed not against the over-scrupulous or the merely careless, but against those who lost their patience after waiting too long in an immense crowd, became distracted and divided in mind, and finally went out in despair. But a great part of the problem has to do with questions of discipline. These are certainly more important than any enforced awe of the real presence. Even now in Eastern churches the great entrance, rather than the communion, is the place for 'fear and trembling'. The communion is by comparison an informal moment. Those who communicate do so standing, except the little children, who are now on most occasions the only communicants. They are in the arms of their parents. Newly baptized babies recall the comparisons of Theodore of Mopsuestia between the natural and the spiritual.[3]

We who by the death of our Lord Christ have received a sacramental birth, ought also to receive by the same death the nourishment of the sacrament of immortality. We must be nourished from the same sources at which we were also born, according to the custom of all living things who from their birth are naturally nourished by those who give birth to them.

[1] Canon 101: Communicants may not receive the sacramental elements in vessels. See my *Byzantine Patriarchate*, p. 30 and refs.
[2] In his third homily on Ephesians, M.P.G. 62, c. 27-30. See W. J. Sparrow-Simpson, *Non-communicating Attendance*, 1913, pp. 107-12.
[3] *Op. cit.*, p. 471.

No doubt the informality is increased by the absence of adult communicants except on great occasions, but the children were always there, always restless, often crying, carried back by their fathers from the mysteries to be nursed at their mothers' breasts. In the time of S. Augustine they were still communicated often not only in Africa but in Rome.[1]

The absence of adults in East and West arises from the problems of sin and penitence.[2] The Church has never been without sinners, who have always known that they ought not to make their communion without repentance. But in the days of persecution those who persisted in serious sin, or gave scandal to the brethren by a solitary but serious lapse from morality, generally disappeared from the Christian company. If they wanted to stay, they could be made penitents, in practice reduced for the time to the ranks of the catechumens, excluded from prayer and the eucharist, but encouraged to attend the church meeting for the readings and the preaching. This however could not be done, at least in the second century, for the three 'capital sins', apostasy, murder and adultery. And no one could be a penitent more than once. Those who committed the 'capital sins', or failed twice, were left to God's mercy. In most cases that did not mean that they stayed lamenting outside the church meeting. They found an easier religion.

This deplorable fact, seldom mentioned by Christian writers,[3] is evident from the problems that ensued when young men and women wanted, and were allowed, to do penance for the sins of the flesh, to the disgust of Tertullian and Hippolytus. Soon a like penance was permitted to those who flinched under severe persecution, to the disgust of Novatian, who made a schism in Rome, and won a considerable following in the other churches.

[1] So it appears from the letter of Pope Innocent I to the African bishops, M.P.L., 20, c. 592. See S. Cyprian, *De lapsis*, c. 25.

[2] For the following paragraphs I have used the documentation in O. D. Watkins, *A History of Penance*, Vol. I, 1920, supplemented by R. C. Mortimer, *The Origins of Private Penance in the Western Church*, Oxford, 1939.

[3] The classical instance is Lucian's Peregrine. So I should interpret the account of the Emperor Philip the Arabian in Eusebius, *Hist. Eccles.*, Bk. vi, c. 34.

But the problems created by new tactics on the part of the government, who in the last great persecutions sought to make apostates rather than martyrs, were as nothing to the difficulties that arose after the reconciliation between church and state in 313, stabilized in East and West after 323. Now that the civic religions were disestablished and breaking up, and even the Mysteries were becoming secretive underground movements, those who wanted religious consolations must find them in the Church, who for the first time was faced with crowds of Christians who repeatedly failed to live up to their baptismal obligations, and yet persisted in remaining Christians. In the past the weaker brethren had simply lapsed, if a single period of penitential treatment did not succeed in putting them straight, but now they had no other refuge. If they were far-sighted, they remained catechumens for as long as they could, and were baptized on their deathbed. If they were baptized in the enthusiasm of youth, they postponed penance knowing that if they fell a second time they were doomed to lifelong excommunication.

It is often said that discipline was relaxed, and this is true in the sense that penitential discipline was not imposed in many cases where in the past it would have been. But it still appears that Christians in large numbers were excluded from communion for long periods, either as penitents in various categories, or as *energumens*, possessed persons, troubled souls who were regarded as diabolical cases, and treated with exorcisms and laying-on-of-hands. These were dismissed with the catechumens, but certain classes of penitents were at least in some of the churches allowed to remain for the prayers and the thanksgiving, although for the time being they were denied communion. These were not penitents in the strict sense, and were not denied penance in this or in the more severe form if they fell again. This milder form of penance was often used, perhaps invented, to cover the frailties of the weaker sex, and from this we may infer that these semi-penitents were not the only Christians present at the thanksgiving without making their communion. Others might join them from scruples of conscience who were never enrolled in their ranks. Many who dared not open their griefs for fear of the older and more rigorous forms of penance might have serious doubts of their own fitness to communicate.

All this is immediately relevant to our purpose only in so far as it contributed to create large congregations of worshippers who were present at the prayers and at the eucharistic thanksgiving, whose offerings could be accepted, as those of catechumens and penitents could not, although they communicated very seldom. They came to believe that the priest perfected their offerings for them. Such congregations were common in all parts of Christendom, but whereas in the East they joined in the litanies and chants, brought their baptized children to communion, and received the bread of the prothesis at the conclusion of the liturgy, in the West they came to watch and pray while a mysterious rite was performed by the priest with the help of a clerk or clerks. To assist at mass in the technical sense was to hear, to be there while the gospel procession gave place to the offering, to wait through the preface and sanctus for the elevation of host and chalice. After the *agnus Dei*, the bell rang again as the priest made his communion. In a few more moments, the congregation were dismissed at the *Ite, missa est*. On the rare occasions of general communion, they would communicate at a side-altar,[1] in one kind after the twelfth century,[2] but not always kneeling. Standing for communion continued in some places until the eve of the Reformation,[3] a relic of the primitive past as the general communion was.

5. PRIESTS AND PEOPLE

This difference between East and West may be summarized by saying that in the East the people thought of themselves as communicants, unless they were under discipline, dismissed with the penitents, even if they did not communicate except in the bread of the prothesis. In the West they thought of themselves as penitents,

---

[1] Jungmann ii, pp. 374-5.   [2] Not invariably, *ibid.*, pp. 385-6.
[3] *Ibid.*, p. 376: 'That the Body of the Lord should be received kneeling is a custom which slowly and gradually gained the ascendancy in the West between the eleventh and sixteenth centuries.'

admitted to communion when they fulfilled their duties after the fast of Lent or the other fast of Advent, reverting to their previous status on the following Sunday. The difference has less to do with the gap between the liturgical and the vernacular language, which was perhaps as large or as slight in the Latin countries in the Middle Ages as it is today in Greece and the Slavonic countries, than with the almost complete absence of a people's part in the Roman mass. The proper chants belong to an occasion, and were therefore proper to the clerks before they were taken over by the priest at low masses. The only invariable chants outside the preface and sanctus were the Kyries, the remains of a litany introduced by the African Pope Gelasius, the *agnus Dei*, introduced by the Syrian Sergius at the end of the seventh century, the *Gloria in excelsis*, for a long time confined to the bishop's mass, and the creed, which was not introduced at Rome until the eleventh century. The solemn collects, the original Roman intercessions, represent the characteristic attitude of Rome to the people's part. The priest prays aloud for the needs of the Church. The deacon cries, 'Let us bow the knee' and 'Arise'. The people pray, but in silence. By contrast the Eastern liturgies are full of familiar and recurring litanies. The constant refrain, *Kyrie eleeson*, could be translated, 'Sir, I beg your pardon'. They have their rhetorical moments, their purple passages, their poetical splendours, contrasting with the sobriety and simplicity of the Roman canon, but also they never lose touch with common speech. In every age they were translated into new vernaculars, into Old Slavonic in the ninth century, into Arabic instead of Syriac in the Middle Ages, in the seventeenth century into Rumanian, in the nineteenth into Tartar languages and into Chinese and Japanese.

Two attempts to bridge the gulf between priest and people in the Middle Ages seem to me instructive. The first is the elevation of the host, which had more to do with the desire to communicate the consecration to the adoring multitudes than with scholastic discussions of the moment. The practice precedes, at least in Paris, the Lateran Council of 1215, where the real presence was defined in terms which include for the first time, the word transubstantiation. And this definition, considered in its historical context, has more to do with the rejection of crudities than with any new emphasis on transformation at the consecration.

The second is the attempt to develop a new dialogue between priest and people at the *Orate fratres*, after the offertory and before the secret collects and the preface. In the first reference to the *Orate fratres* in a Western rite, in a pontifical liturgy of the eighth century, Roman in form but probably not Roman in origin, the appeal for prayer is addressed by the bishop to the concelebrating priests,[1] but in many of the missals of the Middle Ages it is in the form *Orate fratres et sorores*, as at York:[2]

Pray, brethren and sisters, for me a sinner, that the sacrifice, yours as well as mine (*meum pariterque vestrum*), may be accepted of the Lord our God.

At York the choir replies with verses from Psalm xx:

The Lord hear thee in the day of trouble: the name of the God of Jacob defend thee:
Send thee help from the sanctuary: and strengthen thee out of Sion;
Remember all thy offerings: and accept thy burnt-sacrifice.

In *The Lay Folks Mass Book*, a Norman-French manual of devotion translated into English of the thirteenth and fourteenth centuries,[3] prayer for the priest is recommended at this point:

The holy ghost into thee lyghte,
And send into thee right
To rule thy heart and thy speaking
To God's worship and His loving.

The Sarum prayer is that

The grace of the Holy Spirit illuminate thy heart and lips, and that the Lord accept this sacrifice of praise at thy hands, for our sins and offences.

In the Roman rite of the Middle Ages the appeal for prayer was in the form *Orate fratres*, and the reply was, as it now is:

[1] Jungmann, ii, p. 82, n. 1.
[2] Ed. by W. Henderson for the Surtees Society, 1874, p. 171.
[3] Ed. T. F. Simmons, EETS, 1879, pp. 24-5.

The Lord accept the sacrifice at thy hands to the praise and glory of His name, for our benefit, and that of His whole holy Church.

But now it is provided that the priest may reply himself. The form *Orate fratres* need not exclude the laity, but their part is not emphasized.

The very terms of the attempt made to draw the people into the offering can only emphasize the fact that in their eyes and his the sacrifice is the priest's. As Fr Jungmann[1] says:

The priest feels very strongly that he is exalted above the people—a matter the early mediaeval Church was fully conscious of—and even in his sacrificial prayer he realizes he stands alone before God as the people's mediator.

By contrast in some Syrian rites where Fr Jungmann sees equivalents of the *Orate fratres*, the prayer is 'My brethren and my masters, pray for me that my sacrifice be accepted',[2] or 'Pray for me, my brethren and my beloved, that I be accounted worthy'.[3] The accent is entirely different, for the priest about to begin his particular part in the offering turns to his co-offerers, as the primitive bishop might turn to his presbyters.

Nevertheless the mediaeval lay folk did think that they had a part in the offering. They offered their oblations for particular intentions, and especially for the repose of the faithful departed. At this point we return to the widow of Tours,[4] who was as conscious of possession in her oblation of a bottle of wine as the modern Roman Catholic is of his stipend paid for a particular mass. It is this awareness of the people's oblation, and at the same time of the difference between this and the priest's sacrifice, that does something to explain the developing distinctions of the later Middle Ages between prayers of oblation before and after the elevation of the host in the narrative of the institution. The prayers after relate to the *sanctum sacrificium*. Yet this phrase in its context in the canon refers to the sacrifice of Melchisedech, a sacrifice of bread and wine. According to the *Liber Pontificalis*,[5] it was

---

[1] Vol. II, p. 83.   [2] L.E.W., p. 83 (the Syrian Jacobites).
[3] *Ibid.*, p. 272 (East Syrians or Nestorians).
[4] *Supra*, pp. 65-6.   [5] Vol. I, p. 239.

introduced in protest against Manichaeans, which probably means those who depreciate the sacrifices of the Old Testament. Here and elsewhere, as in the offertory prayer, the *immaculatam hostiam* originally means the pure offering, the antitypes accepted and carried to the altar in heaven, that they may be given to us as the Body and Blood of Christ. To this conception of the unity of the entire eucharistic action the modern liturgical movement in the Roman Catholic Church seems to be returning, under the guidance of such theologians as Canon Eugene Masure,[1] and in this there is hope, not only of a reconciliation between East and West, but of an understanding of the doctrine of sacrifice no longer open to objection from the Protestant tradition.

On the Protestant side it must be remembered that that tradition itself is coloured by the inheritance of the Middle Ages. Because mediaeval Christians thought of the eucharistic sacrifice as offered for them by the hands of the priest, who sacrificed and communicated in their place, they thought of the sacrifice of Christ in similar terms. As in the pagan religions mythologies arise to explain rituals, so the Western theology of the atonement was built up to justify and interpret the accepted ways of worship. That Christ died as our substitute in the face of God's wrath is neither a Scriptural nor a primitive notion. Of this the East knew nothing. It is a development to which earlier strands of thought contribute, but its structure belongs to the age of S. Anselm and the Schoolmen. Developed in one direction, in such a way as to concentrate the whole sacrifice in the passion,[2] it produced the explosion of the Reformation, which is essentially a protest against repetition of the passion in the mass.

[1] Especially in *The Sacrifice of the Body*, Eng. trans., 1954.
[2] See G. Dix, *Shape*, pp. 623-4, which is important, and *infra*, note A, pp. 107-11.

CHAPTER FIVE

THE BAPTISMAL SACRIFICE

I. THE CROSS AND THE SACRAMENTS

WITHOUT baptism and the eucharist, the death of Christ would not be reckoned a sacrifice. To those who accept his divine claim, it would still be the greatest crime in history, but what has the death of the Son of God to do with the slaughter of bulls and goats, and of other sacrificial victims in all religions? The sacrificial interpretation of the death of Christ may be rejected, as it often is, on the ground that in our accounts of the last supper Christ is the demon of the year, the spirit of corn and wine, presenting his body and blood to the cultivators of the soil:

... At bottom it is the death of the Kyrios which is specified as the real foundation of the cultic meal when it is attributed to Jesus' last supper, for the body and blood of Jesus distributed by him at this meal are ... in mysterious anticipation the body and blood of the crucified, sacrificed Christ.[1]

The same writer affirms that[2]

In Hellenistic Christianity the Lord's Supper ... is understood *as a sacrament in the sense of the mystery religions* ... Paul himself shows that the sacrament of the Lord's Supper stands in this context in the history of religions.

And[3]

Baptism imparts participation in the death and resurrection of Christ. This interpretation ... originated in the Hellenistic Church, which understood the traditional initiation-sacrament on analogy with the initiation-sacraments of the mystery religions.

This is a possible position to hold, perhaps the only truly consistent position for those who study Christian origins without believing that Jesus Christ is the Son of God in the sense of the

---

[1] R. Bultmann, *The Theology of the New Testament*, Eng. trans., Vol. I, 1952, p. 148.
[2] *Ibid.*   [3] *Op. cit.*, p. 140.

classical creeds. The difficulty is to explain how such an image was integrated into the traditions of a community of Palestinian-Jewish origin when the Church was only beginning to spread beyond the boundaries of Palestine, and to escape from the rigidly iconoclastic traditions of Hebrew religion. Much harder to sustain is the attempt to affirm sacrifice in the crucifixion of Christ, and at the same time to reduce the connection between the sacraments and this sacrifice. In the words of Bishop Rawlinson,[1] words which a Baptist theologian has lately called 'one of the truly seminal sentences in New Testament scholarship':[2]

The doctrine of sacrifice (and of atonement) was not . . . read *into* the Last Supper; it was read out of it. It was the Last Supper which afforded the clue.

There, Dr Rawlinson says:

Interpreting in advance the significance of His coming Passion, He was in effect making it to be, for all time, what it otherwise would not have been, viz.: a sacrifice for the sins of the world. It is the Last Supper which makes Calvary sacrificial.

Those who believe that Christ is indeed the Saviour of the world may reverently conceive him as looking forward into the penumbra of Hellenistic civilization that surrounded Palestine, and knowing this not only as another Passover meal, a new Day of atonement, but as a mystery wherein Jew and Greek could both partake, a common initiation, a bond of communion.

That some connection exists between the atonement and the sacraments is assumed in the classical forms of Protestantism. What is denied is a necessary connection between baptism and incorporation into Christ, between communion with Christ and the eucharist. In a sense no doubt we all deny this, every time when we speak of a baptism of desire, a baptism of blood, and spiritual communion, or say that God 'is not tied to his sacraments'; but the Protestant in the tradition of Geneva and Zurich

---

[1] In *Mysterium Christi*, ed. G. K. A. Bell and A. Deissmann, 1930, p. 241.
[2] N. Clark, in *An Approach to the Theology of the Sacraments*, 1956, p. 63.

would deny that the promises of God can apply to all baptized children, not, as I understand this tradition,[1] because they cannot have any present faith in his name, but because they may have no vocation thereafter to believe on him and to accept his promises. They may be regenerate at the font, but their regeneration is conditional and can only be completed by commitment in later life. And for a like reason, they deny that those who make their communion without such a vocation, confirmed and sealed by confession of their faith, can be made partakers of Christ's Body and Blood. Zwingli and some of the Swiss and English Reformers under his immediate influence went a stage further than this, when they maintained that communion with Christ in prayer and sacrament are of the same kind and in the same mode, for the eucharist is first and last a means whereby Christ is remembered. But this form of Reformed Protestantism did not long survive the robust influence of Calvin. It may be doubted whether it was more than a phase in Zwingli's mental development, so soon cut short by his early death in battle. His view of the Lord's Supper as a pure memorial offering of bread and wine was later revived in association with interpretations of the sacrifice of Christ as metaphor rather than fact, a figure of the love of God, but not a deed wrought for us.

Where the sacrifice of Christ is remembered as an act done, not only a way of revealing love behind what justice moves the world, there belief in a mysterious presence hidden in the outward signs persists, however unwilling men may be to define the mode of the sacramental action, or to nail it down, in any way whatever, to a place or moment. It is my belief that within this area of agreement our differences might be reduced to a much smaller compass, if not annihilated, if we thought of baptism and the eucharist as two parts of one whole complex action, essentially interdependent in the end as in the beginning. In the long contention about regeneration in baptism, already briefly outlined, the supporters

---

[1] I have been much helped by J. B. Mozley's masterly *Survey of the Baptismal Controversy*, written as long ago as 1862, and at other times by G. W. Bromiley, *Baptism and the Anglican Reformers*.

of the doctrine of baptismal regeneration have often forgotten that baptism without the eucharist is incomplete, an unfinished rite. This has led them to misuse patristic testimonies which really refer to the whole transformation that came to a converted and baptized Christian in the course of his catechumenate and after his first communion.[1] On the other hand their Evangelical critics have often supposed, partly for this reason, that to believe baptismal regeneration must be to attribute to every baptized infant that certainty of salvation which we ought all to await in fear and trembling.[2] But it is one thing to affirm with the English Prayer Book that 'Children which are baptized, dying before they commit actual sin, are undoubtedly saved', and another to maintain a difference in fundamental spiritual status between a baptized man who does not know whether he is baptized or not, and does not care a brass farthing one way or the other, and a man uncertain whether he needs to ask for baptism, who desires the baptized life with all his heart. The second, before his conditional baptism, is ready for communion. The first, if his baptism were certain, would not now care to communicate. He might have done so in the days of the Test Act, when a certificate of communion was required for offices. But this would have been a profanation, greater in the eyes of those who insisted on baptismal regeneration than in the minds of moderate churchmen, who saw no certain good in his baptism and no terrible harm in his communion.

2. BAPTISMAL DISCIPLINE

That particular problem is no longer serious in the present age. Our particular problems here in Britain and more especially in the established churches of England and Scotland, relate to the baptism of infants whose parents are vaguely anxious about the many dangers that surround their frail bodies and tempestuous energies. Baptism is commonly regarded as a kind of exorcism, potent against unexpected setbacks, and at least providing some sense of relief if a delicate infant departs lamenting 'to heaven'.

[1] See J. B. Mozley, *op. cit.*, especially pp. 163-77.
[2] *Ibid.*, pp. 111-62.

These beliefs are a trouble to the parish clergy when combined with complete indifference to any other sacramental rite except the burial of the dead and, in less degree, the solemnization of matrimony.

Perhaps the worry is overdone. Firstly, the problem is a residue of a condition of things that in time must pass away, for two outstanding reasons. The decline of infant mortality in the present century seems now on the way to making the individual child's chance of survival so high that in the next generation young parents will cease to be obsessed by the fears left in their minds by the little coffins of their mother's childhood and their grandmother's recollections. Secondly the fear of hell has grown dim among faithful Christians for good and bad reasons and is fading out of existence in the secular world. The limbo of unbaptized infants was not a very terrible place in the Middle Ages, in comparison with the other regions of hell. It may have become more scarifying in some preaching since the Reformation, but I doubt if sermons against the dangers of leaving the baby unbaptized have been preached in many English parish churches in the last sixty years. A hundred years ago the theme was a popular one, when the Gorham judgment was recent, and Tractarians and High Churchmen fought to defend 'one baptism for the remission of sins' against the dangerous leniency of the Judicial Committee of the Privy Council, who on March 8, 1850, allowed that a clergyman of England might be permitted to believe

That Baptism is a Sacrament generally necessary to salvation, but that the grace of regeneration does not so necessarily accompany the act of Baptism that regeneration invariably takes place in Baptism; that the grace may be granted before, in, or after Baptism . . . That infants baptized, and dying before actual sin, are certainly saved but that in no case is regeneration in Baptism unconditional.[1]

It must be remembered that Bishop Phillpotts of Exeter, who was the High Church protagonist in the Gorham case, had a few years before thrown the cloak of his moral protection over a priest prosecuted and convicted in the Ecclesiastical Courts for refusing

[1] Quoted in J. C. S. Nias, *Gorham and the Bishop of Exeter*, 1951, p. 98.

to bury in his churchyard a child baptized by a Methodist lay preacher.[1] Many High Churchmen of his generation denied the validity of lay baptism. The priest who refused to bury Tess's baby in consecrated ground may, when Hardy wrote, have been rather old-fashioned, but twenty years before he was a common figure. The memory of clergy who refused Christian burial in any form to unbaptized infants, or to those baptized by laymen, who in their eyes included lay preachers and Methodist ministers, lies behind a great deal of obstinate anti-clericalism in English towns and villages. It also accounts for something more positive, the persistence of grandmothers in avoiding such embarrassments by insisting that the baby must be 'done'.

Moreover it ought not to be forgotten that one who is now regarded by many as the greatest English theologian of the nineteenth century, F. D. Maurice, had to face obloquy from the Evangelical and High Church parties, including the Tractarians, because he insisted that Christ on the cross had redeemed the whole human race, not the elect, and not individual baptized persons, that in him the baptized are incorporated into redeemed mankind, and so saved from their own individualism. This may not be in the strict sense traditional doctrine, but it is certainly easier to reconcile with the baptismal practice and tradition of the Church than the belief that some, the called, but not others, the rejected, receive regeneration in the baptismal waters. Maurice saw baptism as a rite that 'receives men into the holy Communion of saints', not one 'that bestows upon them certain individual blessings, endows them with a certain individual holiness'.[2] Because Christ is and lives and has taken humanity to himself we are in him. We have to become what we are.

Of this engrafting into Christ of which Maurice speaks in the very language of the Christian Fathers, baptism is the proper beginning, but not the end (unless the course be interrupted by immediate death, as in former years it so often was in the case of

---

[1] See his *Charge to the clergy of the diocese . . .*, 1842, on this and on Tract XC.
[2] *The Kingdom of Christ*, 3rd ed., 1883, Vol. I, p. 340.

infants). An uncompleted baptism may be reckoned no more than a beginning. It is not a false start, for a man baptized in infancy and converted in maturity has no need to be rebaptized, but it is no more than the first move.

Those who think that to make this move without any prospect of future progress is mocking God and worse than useless, set out to devise safeguards, but these generally amount to little more than protection for themselves from direct complicity. It seems a small comfort not to have baptized a baby who may be baptized by his grandmother in a bowl of water on the kitchen table. At a later stage in life the boy or girl may have to wrestle with his mother's fierce hostility to the clergy and his own uncertainty about his own position. Was he baptized at all, and when ? That in our secular world the majority of children may never reflect on the matter will not lessen the sensitiveness of some, who may be more numerous since the quality of religious teaching has improved in all our schools, and religious questions are constantly raised in the minds of those brought up in secular homes.

Better than a negative refusal, which in any case would not be supported by all the neighbouring parishes, still less by other communions practising infant baptism in the same district, would be a steady insistence that the public baptism of infants is part of the public prayer of the Church, and ought to take place as part of her public liturgy. This is easier for the Church of Scotland and for those English communions whose worship has no fixed liturgical form, than for the Church of England, whose rubrics provide for baptisms at only two alternative places, after the second lesson at Morning or Evening Prayer. But in this a larger liberty may be granted, or alternative arrangements made in projects for the revision of the Prayer Book that are already in hand. And even in our present situation a large liberty of omission is in practice given, which could enable us after a baptism to dispense with the rest of Morning Prayer and some part of the Order of Communion, that the two gospel sacraments might be seen in close integration.

It may be hazardous for a writer without parochial experience to make a practical suggestion, but I think something could be done without archaism towards a revival of the scrutinies before baptism. If, as we are told, baptism is commonly regarded as a prophylactic against dim and dangerous evils, the continual prayer of the Church that the child may be delivered from the malignities of the devil's devices might be better understood if these were specifically enumerated in a distinct rite. The ceremonial need not be elaborate, and the language should take account of the fears and temptations of our own age, when demons take the form of obsessions, and sin is conceived in a dim fashion under the darkness of multiple perversions. Children taken in the arms of an officer of the Church, and prayed for in some special fashion at home as well as in the church, might have a better chance of engaging the sympathies of the whole congregation, into which their hesitating parents might be drawn, so that when the time came they might see baptism as incorporation into Christ, and not only another exorcism. If on the other hand they disliked engaging the forces of evil, and preferred to be neutral, they would probably withdraw before the day of decision, leaving the child unbaptized, the sacrament unprofaned.

The obstacles to such proceedings may be found not so much in the unwillingness of the parents to attend a public service, or even two such services, where Selina Caroline is a focus of attention, as in the objections of some members of the congregation to interruptions in the ordinary course of the public liturgy for such newcomers as Selina Caroline. For this reason it might be wise to make the first part of the Publick Baptism of Infants, corresponding to the making of a catechumen, into a separate office for parents and godparents, family and friends, either in the home or at the church before the public service. But the blessing of the water in the font, baptism in the threefold name, and sealing with the sign of the cross, ought to be an integral part of the eucharistic liturgy. Their precise placing is a practical problem, which will be considered further in the next section. The position prescribed in the Prayer Book after the second lesson at Morning Prayer has this advantage, when the eucharist follows, that the focus of attention need not shift to and fro between the altar and the font. But baptism at an evening service is neither practical nor edifying. Very few parents want their children baptized at bedtime.

3. THE ANGLICAN EUCHARIST

The whole question of the constant relation of the eucharist to the *synaxis*, the gathering of the church for prayer and preaching, is relevant to the subject of this book because if it is insisted that every eucharist must have preaching, and a full complement of readings and prayers, it will obviously be difficult either to baptize infants, or adult catechumens, in a eucharistic setting, or to integrate other initiations, such as marriage and the acceptance of other serious responsibilities, with the eucharistic worship of the Church.

On the one hand it is held by some that a eucharist without preaching is mutilated, almost invalid, and by others that while the brief readings of the epistle and gospel are sufficient, these, with the prayer for the Church, ought never to be omitted. The whole question of the essentials of the *synaxis*, and of omissions from this, requires examination. In this and the following paragraphs, I shall speak as an Anglican to Anglicans, believing that all English Christians have reason to be concerned with the future of liturgical worship in the Church of England.

The Anglican *synaxis* in its prescribed form, laid down in the rubrics, consists of Morning Prayer, the Litany (in full), the Our Father and collect for purity, the ten commandments, two collects (one for the Queen), sometimes three, the epistle and gospel, the creed and sermon, and the prayer for the Church militant. In the present pace of modern life this is too much, but in our attempts to abbreviate, we have too often omitted the wrong things. Either Morning Prayer is pushed into a corner, or in some other quarters the first part of the Communion office is omitted altogether. The Litany, whose literary excellence is admitted on every side, seems now to be in the course of complete disappearance from public worship, and this is a calamity, for unlike our other intercessions, it is not a monologue to be recited by the priest alone, while the rest, in the old Roman fashion, mutter an Amen.

It would be more rational, as it seems to me, to consider the morning service as a whole, and eliminate unnecessary repetitions. The responses at the end of Morning Prayer, beginning with 'Lord have mercy upon us', might well be regarded as a shorter version of the great intercession in the Litany beginning

We sinners do beseech thee to hear us, O Lord God: and that it may please thee to rule and govern thy holy Church universal in the right way.

This has its anachronisms, e.g. 'the Lords of the Council and all the nobility', but no more than the prayer for the Church militant. If the responses at the end of Morning Prayer or this part of the Litany (to the Our Father) were recited before the collects at a celebration of the eucharist, and preceded by Morning Prayer to the *Te Deum*, it would be reasonable to omit the prayer for the Church before the great eucharistic thanksgiving, whereas now in so many Anglican churches this stands between the first oblation of the elements and 'Lift up your hearts'.

This anomaly has arisen in part through a misinterpretation of the place of the prayer for the Church militant in the order of the Book of Common Prayer. In the old Anglican tradition this is the last prayer of the Antecommunion. The rubric for the preparation of the elements was put before it in 1662 to settle a question left open in previous Prayer Books since 1549 but without any intention of making this the offertory in the original sense of the taking of the sacramental elements for consecration. As Bishop Dowden proved, in arguments that have never been refuted, 'alms and oblations' in the prayer for the Church refer to two kinds of collections.[1] The offertory sentences all refer to such alms and oblations, not to the sacramental elements. The rubric before the prayer for the Church refers simply to the prothesis, corresponding to the preparation of the elements in the Sarum rite after the introit, in the Dominican high mass between the epistle and the gospel, in the Eastern liturgies before the readings. The prayer for the Church militant ought

---

[1] In an article on 'Our alms and oblations' in JTS, Vol. I, 1900, pp. 321-46, reprinted in *Further Studies in the Prayer Book*, 1908, pp. 176-223.

not to be considered as a detached part of the prayer of consecration. It is true that it was included in this prayer in the liturgy of 1549, but there it is an awkward interruption between the sanctus and the commemoration of redemption. It may reasonably be conjectured that it was intended for another place, perhaps its present one, and included in the canon in deference to conservative misgivings. In any case it is now a part of the antecommunion, and should be regarded as a final intercession repeating the intercessions of the lesser and greater litanies at the end of Morning Prayer.

The real offertory of the Anglican rite is in another rubric, after the prayer of humble access:

When the priest, standing before the table, hath so ordered the Bread and Wine, that he may with the more readiness and decency break the bread before the people, and take the cup into his hands, he shall say the prayer of consecration, as followeth:

This, and this alone, corresponds to the direction in the *Apostolic Tradition*:

To him let the deacons bring the oblation and he with all the presbyters laying his hand on the oblation shall say giving thanks: 'The Lord be with you'.[1]

Its present placing reflects the practice of Bishop Andrewes, who in an interleaved Prayer Book of his own[2] provided directions for the priest to wash his hands and to prepare the elements at this point.

Postremo omnibus rite, et quam fieri potest, decentissime et aptissime compositis, stans pergit et peragit.

His practice was probably followed by others, and his words have evidently influenced the language of the rubric. But this practice was based on a misunderstanding, common in his time, of the relation between the preface and sanctus and the rest of the prayer

---

[1] P. 6.

[2] See his works in the *Library of Anglo-Catholic Theology*, Vol. XI, p. 157, and my article on 'Offertory and Oblation' in *Theology* Vol. IX, 1957, pp. 327-9.

of consecration, which in the mediaeval manuscripts, and in the early printed missals, was distinguished as the CANON in the proper sense. The same traditional misconception led to the placing of the prayer of humble access after the sanctus in 1552, and its retention in the same place in 1662, when liturgical studies were reviving, but had not yet gone far enough to reveal the *rationale* of the primitive prayer of thanksgiving. If the prayer of humble access were removed from the midst of the prayer of consecration, and placed before the communion, as in the Prayer Book of 1549, or with the offertory before 'Lift up your hearts' as in the proposals for the revision of the Prayer Book in 1927, the eucharistic thanksgiving in the Anglican liturgy would be at least in harmony with the outline of the universal primitive pattern.

In the preface and sanctus God is glorified for his own being, and for the gifts of creation. The commemoration of redemption follows, concluding 'until his coming again'. What comes after corresponds, not to the narrative of the institution in the ancient liturgies, for this has already been summarized, but to the *post-mysterium*, the *anamnesis* and prayer for the unity of the Church through her communion in the Body and Blood of Christ. In 1549 this included an *epiclesis* and a fuller *anamnesis*, but since 1552 and 1559 the *anamnesis*

According to thy Son our Saviour Jesus Christ's holy institution, in remembrance of his death and passion

has come to a final conclusion in words whereby 'the consecration is consummated' according to the tradition common to the Reformers, the parish priests who first used the Prayer Books, and the people who answered them with an Amen.[1]

The eucharistic thanksgiving is the common prayer of the baptized people of God, offering themselves with their symbolic oblations to God the Father, Son, and Holy Ghost. In the old Anglican tradition, preserved into the present century in some

---

[1] See Innocent III as cited *supra*, p. 77. The passage was quoted in the *Rationale divinorum officiorum* of Durandus (c. 1296), f. lxxvi *verso* of the Lyons ed., 1506. Cranmer's copy of this is in the British Museum.

country parishes, and still today in Methodist churches,[1] all stood
to say or sing not only the sanctus, but 'Therefore with angels and
archangels . . .' The priest's part is important, because he has
authority, however derived, from the whole Church. He is not
simply the spokesman of a particular congregation, but his sacrifice and the people's are one and the same. (He said in the *York
Missal* in mediaeval days, *meum pariterque vestrum*.[2]) What is
offered does indeed include ourselves, our souls and bodies, but
ourselves built up into the Body of Christ. Therefore it seems a
mistake to lay a special emphasis on our alms and oblations in
association with the preparation of the elements, unless this is
closely integrated with the preparation of the communicants, and
with the whole eucharistic action.[3] If it were, this would be the
proper place for baptism, confirmation, and other solemn dedications. In the Roman mass, where prothesis and offertory are bound
together, and close to the consecration, an offertory procession
helps to integrate the oblations of the people with the eucharistic
sacrifice. But an offertory procession before the prayer for the
Church can have the opposite effect.

4. THE CONTEMPORARY PROBLEM

Our present problems are different from those of the primitive
Church, different in that we all have to minister to people with
Christian traditions, whose natural religious feelings run in Christian channels, and are always in danger of transforming revealed
into natural religion. Even in the mission field many converts have
been drawn to the Christian faith in the first place because it
provides the one religious interpretation of the new culture that
has reached their shores, and is in the course of permeating the
practical pattern of their lives. Therefore we cannot afford to be
archaists. If we endure persecution, we engage in a struggle

---

[1] In Methodist usage all stand for the 'comfortable words', and kneel
at the prayer of humble access.

[2] P. 171, cited *supra*, p. 89.

[3] This is recommended in the report of the sub-committee on The Book
of Common Prayer in the report of *The Lambeth Conference*, 1958,
p. 281.

between rival interpretations of the same modern, post-Christian civilization. Is the belief that material things are important, and the succession of historical events no illusion but more significant than the flight of the alone to the alone—is this bound up with belief in the incarnation, or is it rather an end-product of the long Christian warfare against natural religion ? Is the Christian faith merely a stage in man's emancipation from idols, or is man certain to fall again under the dominion of demonic powers if he rejects the gospel of Christ ?

This is the true issue of our time, often obscured for Christians by the illusion that our religion needs defences against materialism or even against science. We ought rather to claim the modern occupation with material improvements as the most important practical legacy of Christian charity to European thinking and action. It is also obscured by the common belief that the sacrifice of Christ is so completely different from all other sacrifices in other religions that the Christian faith has more in common with such higher religions as Buddhism and Islam, where there are no proper sacrifices, than with the lower religions of soil and sex. But the opposite is the case; they too are means whereby man learns to live, not as an isolated individual, pursuing his spiritual pilgrimage from the alone to the alone, but as 'a member of Christ, a child of God, and an inheritor of the kingdom of heaven'. The higher religions may be what man does with his solitude, but the Christian faith is the gift of communion with God.

In this book we begin with the lower religions, with rites of initiation and sacrifice that may not even assume a personal god, but nevertheless accept the necessity of death for the all-devouring, self-regarding, insatiable infant, that the child may mature in company, and become in time a member of a society linking the living and the dead with the unborn who are still to be. If, as I am inclined to believe, the dim recognition of such a necessity lies behind the continued anxieties of families who do not practise the Christian religion, not only about the baptism of their children, but about the due performance of 'the thanksgiving of women after child-birth, commonly called the Churching of women', the scientific study of their nature and history is relevant to the pastoral problems of baptismal discipline. Such anxieties ought not to be dismissed as mere superstition, but interpreted in relation to the Christian doctrine of sin, that they may be relieved by the Christian vision of baptism and the eucharist as communion in the death and resurrection of Christ, an historical death and triumph once completed, once begun in us, but renewed day by day, not only in the eucharist, but in every response to Christ's calling: to leave father and mother and to cleave to a wife, to leave all for the service of Christ, or to accept a special task, near or far, among Aborigines in Arnhemland or factory workers on the Great West Road. But the understanding of this depends in the first place on our understanding of the eucharist, not as a repetition or reiteration of the sacrifice of Christ, but as the sacramental means whereby his death and resurrection, and our baptism, are renewed in us.

NOTE

Page 91: Poena vicaria

THIS is not a history of the doctrine of the atonement, but I am aware that I shall be challenged for saying again, as I did in *Lamb to the Slaughter*,[1] that the developed doctrine of satisfaction made to the wrath of God for the sin of man by the vicarious penal suffering of the innocent Christ is a product of mediaeval reflection on the cross in the context of the mass, and more especially of low mass, where the priest alone offers and communicates on behalf of others who are either absent or 'assist' at a distance a rite completed in a language other than their own.

First on the matter of date: the article on the atonement in the *Schaff-Herzog Encyclopaedia of Religious Knowledge*, New York, 1891, Vol. I, pp. 165-6, by A. H. Hodge, while indeed claiming that 'the Fathers . . . adhered to the sacrificial language of the Old Testament, and to the terms used by the apostles in the New Testament', allows that 'they failed to express their views definitely, or to maintain them consistently'. . . . 'The view which had been implicitly received by the Fathers was first scientifically defined by Anselm, (d. 1109) . . . in his epoch-making book, *Cur Deus Homo?* The "Reformers before the Reformation", e.g. Wycliffe (d. 1384) and John Wessel (d. 1489) and the ancient Waldenses, held the strict Anselmic doctrine.' The author goes on to maintain that 'this has subsequently been adopted in the creeds of the entire Christian Church', but he gives nothing from the East, where the learned and eirenical Dominican, Père Yves Congar, maintains that 'the word satisfaction is not, or scarcely ever is, in the Greek vocabulary'. After enlarging on the consequences of this for the conceptions of penitence and *poena*, penal suffering, he adds a note: 'I believe for my part that this point is very important, and marks the true difference between Eastern

[1] 1957, pp. 115-21.

thought and our own.'[1] This observation should lead us to qualify generalizations as to the presence of ideas similar to the later Western doctrine in the Fathers, especially the Greek Fathers, who thought of substitution rather in terms of a traditional sacrificial vocabulary in which the priest and the victim, each in their action and suffering, represent the offerers and the divinity, and the sacrifice is accomplished through the due performance of the entire rite. From this point of view Christ is indeed the perfect priest and the perfect sacrifice, but his sacrifice includes his whole obedience, and is continued in heaven.

These sacrificial categories were preserved in the East through the liturgy, but lost in the West through the decay of liturgical life, so that when the idea of sacrifice was challenged, as it was in the eleventh and twelfth centuries by the presence at the gates of Christendom of an immensely powerful and cultivated Islamic civilization, others had to be improvised. In these categories the debates of Catholics and Protestants have been conducted in almost every instance until well within the last forty years. The Rev. Nathaniel Dimock was a controversialist of no mean reputation, and of considerable learning, belonging to the Evangelical party in the Church of England, who between 1871 and 1903 combated in a weighty series of writings Anglo-Catholic attempts to revive the idea of a sacrifice in the eucharist. In one in particular, published in 1896, he collected *Testimonies of English Divines in respect of the claim of the 'Massing-Priests' to offer Christ for the quick and dead to have remission of pain or guilt*, and included an *excursus* on certain Roman Catholic divines whose doctrine appeared to resemble what he himself approved. In this[2] he distinguished with care between 'two distinct senses of the verb "to offer" '. With Archbishop Wake[3] and many more, he would allow that in the eucharist 'this presenting to God Almighty this sacrifice of our blessed Lord is a most effectual manner of applying His merits to us'. But this sense, he maintained, 'naturally *implies* the Real Absence'.[4] The other sense of the verb, 'to offer', 'to

[1] In *L'Église et les églises*, the *festschrift* for Dom Lambert Beauduin, editions de Chevetogne, 1954, pp. 35-6.
[2] Pp. 228-36.   [3] Quoted on p. 229.   [4] P. 231.

signify the real sacrificial oblation of the *hostia* to God the Father on the visible altar by the action (in some sort) of the priest then and there . . . requires the Real Presence (in the Romish sense) *sub speciebus*'. For this reason he found a 'strange inconsistency' in the writings of Cardinal Franzelin:[1]

It is impossible to conceive or desire anything more satisfactory than Franzelin's teaching of the one atonement by the one perfect sacrifice, oblation and satisfaction, made by Christ on the cross. . . . It is impossible to read it without thankfulness for his faithful testimony to this truth. Indeed, *so far* it might well be desired that all Protestant theologians had given by their trumpets so certain a sound.

And consistently with this we find him speaking of the Eucharistic *offering* as the offering in representation and exhibition of the perfect sacrifice *once offered*.

Nevertheless, he finds elsewhere in Franzelin a real reiteration of the sacrifice of Christ in the eucharist by the 'exinanitio' of Christ's Body in the transubstantiation.

Such an 'exinanitio' must be understood in order to express the absolute majesty of God's dominion, and the satisfaction for all our sins completed in death, that it may be truly and properly sacrificial.

Thus for Dimock and for Cardinal Franzelin, exinanition or destruction made the mass a true, and not only a representative sacrifice. But according to the modern school of French theologians who began when Louis Billot 'in his teaching at the Roman College . . . with a determined gesture . . . swept away the accumulated rubbish of fruitless controversies'[2] sometime in the eighteen-nineties, there is no new immolation of Christ in the eucharist, and yet the eucharist is a sacrifice. According to Masure[3]

Today the system of Lugo-Franzelin survives only in a disguised form and is almost unrecognizable among its few partisans who hold that the immolation of Christ consists in His being reduced to the state of food and drink.

[1] Pp. 232-5.
[2] E. Masure, *The Christian Sacrifice*, Eng. trans., 1944, p. 226. For the impact of Anglican divines on Billot, see E. Bishop in *Narsai*, p. 136 and note.
[3] In *The Sacrifice of the Body*, p. 15, n. 1.

What has happened between the days of Franzelin whose school 'was flourishing under the same roof where Fr Billot himself was teaching', and the present day is common to all Christian traditions. If the theology of De La Taille and Masure would hardly have been regarded as orthodox in the Roman schools of the eighteen-eighties, Dimock, could he return from the dead, would be much more horrified by Professor C. H. Dodd[1] and Professor C. F. D. Moule.[2] The whole conception of sacrifice has changed under the influence of the modern science of comparative religion, which is as evident in Masure's pages as it is in critical studies of the Old Testament. The important theological divisions of our time relate to this. Cutting across the Protestant-Catholic cleavage they unite the Roman Catholic critics of post-Reformation eucharistic theology with the Protestant critics of the doctrine of Christ's vicarious penal suffering.

So far however Roman Catholic critics have shown a certain natural hesitation and reserve in exploring the historical sources of those theological tendencies which they wish to revise in their own communion, except where an opportunity offers to put some of the blame on a discredited figure such as Ockham, or on the Jansenists. The liturgical limitations of the Middle Ages are admitted, but the theological implications of these have not, so far as I know, been fully expounded. Nothing however seems to be clearer in the general history of religions, than that liturgy is the source of theology as truly as it is the expression of theological ideas. The few strictly theological developments of the Middle Ages, in the doctrine of the atonement, and in the doctrine of the sacraments, were liturgically conditioned if only by the limitations of liturgy. This made questions and answers turn, where the sacraments are concerned, upon due matter and form, and in the sacrifice of Christ on its infinite effect in comparison with our own paltry offering, thereby miraculously transformed into his Body and Blood.

In this there is, and was, a hard core of Evangelical truth. The

---

[1] E.g. in *The Bible and the Greeks*, 1935, pp. 82-95.
[2] In *The Sacrifice of Christ*, 1956.

danger is, here and always, that we reduce God to the measure of ourselves. When Dimock compares, 'with reverent caution' . . . 'the offering of the sacrifice to view' to 'the displaying of the voucher of an account paid',[1] he seems to me to have done just this, in succession to all who had followed and developed S. Anselm's metaphor of a *debitum*, a due, a debt. To S. Anselm, I believe, this meant in the first place a feudal due, a debt of service, but in the debates of his own time the notion of a financial transaction already appears. I cannot but believe that the undue prominence of the idea of payment in the scholastic discussions of sacrifice before and after the Reformation was due partly to the complexity of ecclesiastical finances in the Middle Ages, when the church was far more highly organized than the feudal lordships which in most places provided the only effective civil government, and partly to the influence of the Old Testament on the theologians.

Those of us who are accustomed to study the Scriptures in the light of modern studies in the history of religion may have difficulty in appreciating the impact of the Levitical ordinances considered in themselves on theologians who saw the bulls and goats on the one hand as shadows of good things to come, on the other as oblations made to God and his priests. Blood to them meant death, and the precious blood of Christ the blood of his death, not of his risen life. Therefore the eucharist had to be either in some sense the re-crucifixion of Christ, or the memory of his death. In the words of H. C. G. Moule, another noted Evangelical theologian at the beginning of this century, what Christ gives us is—'we must not shrink from the meaning—His body as dead'.[2] From this conviction common to so much post-Reformation theology, Catholic as well as Protestant, we have been delivered through a deeper study of the idea of sacrifice in all religion.

[1] *Op. cit.*, p. 236.
[2] In the *Report of a Conference held at Fulham Palace in October 1900* (between Anglican theologians), ed. H. Wace, p. 50.

INDEX